ENDORSEMENTS

"This book is a hope-filled journey about how to overcome great personal adversity to live a life that is rich and fulfilling. The book begins with Merrylyn's own journey through grief and loss: Her attitude of calm fortitude is distilled in every sentence, and is an inspiring guide.

Merrylyn passes on her rich wisdom to the reader to apply the lessons to themselves, yet her account is much more than her personal story. As a highly experienced social scientist and researcher, Merrylyn shares deep insights into what people can do to overcome loss and sadness in their lives and replace them with hope and acceptance. The power to author the next part of our lives using these insights is a wonderful gift.

— Dr Karen Morley. Executive Coach, Author, & Speaker

Merrylyn has given us a gift by sharing such a personal story with immense honesty. It is shared with us to offer hope and a way forward when confronted with seemingly unbearable grief. It is easy and challenging to read all at the same time as we recognise the unthinkable pain of the loss of her only son and only biological grandson. Merrylyn emphasises the importance of relationship with yourself and others as you grieve and provides thoughtful strategies about how to achieve this.

This is a book I would recommend to anyone struggling with loss and grief. It can be read as a whole but I am sure readers will also keep coming back to specific chapters to familiarise themselves again with the helpful and compassionate guidance Merrylyn provides along the way.

— Dr. Prue McEvoy, Child and Adolescent Psychiatrist: Lead Psychiatric Director; Department of Child Protection Adelaide

This is the most glorious celebration of self-determination and work and resilience and love. Profoundly sorrowful. Absolutely loving and positive. Thank you for writing this. Just extraordinary. You are a wonderful writer. I love it. I'm honoured to have read your book.
Vanessa Lindsay Barrister

A book of you Merry. Of cruel loss and reflective, insightful hope and recovery. Brave and so much more.

— Roslyn Herring. Good Friend and Great Mah Jong Leader and Participant/Organiser

A book told with compassion and understanding, from the perspective of a well-respected Child and Family Consultant. Merrylyn offers insight into the sensitive and heart-breaking topic of loss through the eyes of someone who has experienced the pain of grief herself. A positive book that holds the reader's hand while helping them find the way forward. I recommend it to anyone who is struggling with the death of a loved one or undergoing personal struggles associated with trauma and shock.

– Barbara Ivusic, Professional Editor – New Author Literary Services

Living, Grieving and Finding Acceptance *is a story of resilience, acceptance and commitment in the face of repeated loss. It serves as a manual for the hard-fought journey from being overwhelmed by grief to finding a balance between honouring the need to grieve and the need to remain open to the many sources of love and gratitude that remain in the world. As such it should prove invaluable not just to those who have suffered loss but also to anyone that wishes to successfully navigate the uncertainties of the current age.*

— Tarrant Cummins PhD (Psychology)

Living, Grieving, and Finding Acceptance

DR MERRYLYN ASQUITH

ABOUT THE AUTHOR

Merrylyn Asquith PhD completed a doctoral thesis in the health and social sciences and was educated in Adelaide. She has written several peer reviewed published articles as well as self-published articles. Over many years, Merrylyn has been dedicated to writing countless reports which have focussed on children's best interests. Merrylyn has worked since 2004 doing the above work in the Family Law Courts, and then as a private practitioner until 2020. She enjoys writing, reading, and researching, and playing Mah Jong with a group of good friends; together with delightful past times like every-day walking, and dinner with friends and family members.

Published in Australia by Sid Harta Publishers Pty Ltd,
ABN: 46 119 415 842
23 Stirling Crescent, Glen Waverley, Victoria 3150 Australia
Telephone: +61 3 9560 9920, Facsimile: +61 3 9545 1742
E-mail: author@sidharta.com.au

First published in Australia 2021   This edition published 2022
Copyright © Dr Merrylyn Asquith 2022
Cover design, typesetting: WorkingType (www.workingtype.com.au)

The right of Dr Merrylyn Asquith to be identified as the Author of the Work has been asserted in accordance with the Copyright, Designs and Patents Act 1988.

Dr Merrylyn Asquith
Living, Grieving, and Finding Acceptance
ISBN: 978-1-925707-70-0 pp152

DEDICATION

This work is dedicated to my beloved boys — forever gone, but in my heart forever. And to all who have experienced extreme trauma and who have freed themselves from negative energy thinking and associated behaviour patterns by developing and understanding their purpose is to grow positivity and happiness. To those who accept their responsibilities to self, and who have worked daily to rise up again. I also dedicate the book to all of those who will, with the help of this book, rise up again.

ACKNOWLEDGEMENTS

Acknowledgements must be directed to Kerry Collison –
Publisher extraordinaire, sturdily practical and informative;
Barbara Ivusic — Editor Extraordinaire *and* a superb,
thoughtful communicator; all of the contributing people at
Sid Harta Publishers; my valued and treasured husband and
all wonderful extended family some of whom have been
fantastic early manuscript readers; the brilliant endorsement
writers whom I treasure for their wit, analysis, bravery and
commitment; and everyone who has supported me along the
sometimes-perilous way of this healing journey. Special thanks
to Michael De Boo and Eliza Clarke for their generous and
very useful reading, suggestions and constant welcome support.

I, Merrylyn Asquith, acknowledge the Kaurna people as
the traditional owners and custodians of the country that I
live and work upon and I pay my respects to other regions
in which I travel.

TABLE OF CONTENTS:

If you require help or if you know someone who needs help, please ring one of the following:

Police in Australia	000
Lifeline	13 11 14
Kids' Helpline	1800 551 800
Men's Line Australia	1300 789 978
Suicide Call Back Service	1300 659 467
Beyond Blue	1300 224 636
Headspace	1800 650 890
ReachOut at	au.reachout.com
Sane Australia	1800187263
QLife	1800184527
Care Leavers Australia (Clan)	1800 008 774

PROLOGUE

At nearly midnight, I was informed that my only son Luke had been murdered. There I was, locked into my sense of his death coupled with impending doom, fate and disaster. I couldn't speak to anyone by phone or in person. On the nights following, my sense of being and every feeling knotted and scrabbled at the slightest whisper. The innocent screeching sulphur crested cockatoo was doing the shrieking for me from his nearby treetop. I could hear the neighbour's son's car pulling into their gravel driveway. I listened to the distant rattle of the train.

And through all of those following nights, there was a black cutting edge to the tolling in my head. If I could have gone with my only son, in those repetitive instants and moments, I would gladly have done so. I could not get over the senselessness of his death, the unfairness, the loss, the cruelty involved.

Over the next few nights, I had rapid, shadowy nightmares. I was in the car with Luke, I saw him smiling next to me. I woke without realising my dream of seeing and loving him. I dreamed many times of Luke flying through the air towards the car. In my dream I reached out to him, the windscreen developed a hole, and Luke reached out to me. I was straining to hold his hand but was unable to reach him.

Then, eleven years later there I was, locked again into my sense of catastrophe and ugly realisation against all odds, of another doomsday, another fateful death and another disaster. What was happening to me?

This disaster had no dreaming attached, but only cold hard reality. It left my son's only son, my precious grandson James, at nineteen years of age, fatally injured in a motorbike accident. My head was again filled with suffering and pain.

It brought with it the remembered suffering and pain at the loss of Luke. And now James; my beautiful boy, a death of my loved one yet again, for what purpose? I wanted escapism, an alternate universe.

How could I go on? What could I do? Where could I go? Who could help me? How could I recover?

INTRODUCTION

N ow I write these words primarily for myself and for anyone who might want to discover, following trauma, how to make life-affirming choices towards lifelong happiness, self-respect and self-love. If, however, satisfaction abounds in your life and you are a contented, grateful, joyful, happy person, this book could still be of interest to you. This book is for all those who would like to be happy each and every day and for those who might not be able to figure out how to be happy, or perhaps, just struggle to get there.

But be warned, what is written here will have much in it that could be quite confronting. Readers will interpret these words based on their culture, values, beliefs, prejudices and life experiences. It helps, I perceive, to extend all viewpoints and try to hold together two or more seemingly differing ideas as true simultaneously. For example, I have determined that I will continue to accept the death of my boys, that it is natural when I grieve their loss and that I am also simultaneously acknowledging making every effort in moving forward.

Throughout this book I talk about why choices must be made. For example, why I choose not to travel endlessly down the grief path. Why I refuse to choose other futile movements towards self-destructive choices, for example diving into drugs or alcohol, which can only bring unhappiness with unhappiness's cousin, accompanying ill health. I also seek to share ways in which a traumatised person, crushed by unforeseen and uncontrollable forces, like my previous self, might work towards increasing understanding. And I seek to share why I choose to build positive emotions while simultaneously choosing to work towards decreasing negative emotions.

You might soon realise, similarly to myself, that what you do and what you choose not to do, are of importance. Our thoughts and actions are a portrayal of the impulsive and lively landscape of our internal and external worlds. We seem to be in the sunlight and then in the darkness. At times we might feel directionless and discover only confusion about which way to go, or which choice to make.

I have found that for myself, over time and with patience, I choose the light. I choose to believe that positive emotions grow optimism, and a constancy of optimism grows resilience against negativity, sadness, hopelessness and fear. I have built a depository of strategies and tactics to draw from. I am always mindful of accepting the reality that something further distressing may occur in the future. I acknowledge to myself that I will need to regulate my emotions as they fluctuate with any untoward circumstance. I accept that I am, ultimately, the one who is in charge of my emotions.

However, throughout this work, I describe how I needed to make unflinchingly difficult and straight-to-the-point challenges for myself as I struggled to stop trying to change;

that is, unrealistically change, the world I was in. This was before I woke up to reality and the awareness of making my own choices. I needed to build a precious store of transformative power within my mind.

Previously to working towards change, I was living in a world where I had viewed and experienced external forces as being beyond my control. I understood that such behaviour was not consistent with my work towards trying to develop ways forward. I had to consciously shake off old and deeply entrenched views and feelings. Over time I came to understand that only I could directly impact and determine my happiness and wellbeing. I gradually moved on and commenced to learn how to have insightful conversations with myself by being quiet and deeply thoughtful in my thinking. I welcomed spontaneously-arising differing and challenging views of the problems I perceived needed addressing.

- *Take a chance to evaluate your life and life choices while you understand that everyone is poles apart in their life opportunities and capacities. This self-examination is your opportunity to better determine the outcomes you desire and the choices necessary to get there. A first step along the way to personal mastery of self.*

- *Acknowledge that everyone is essentially different in their approach to the present, the past and the future. Fortunate people may recall their lives with gratitude, and remember their delightful childhoods, life opportunities and so on. Others, for any number of reasons, have not had those life-enhancing experiences. Your approach is the one you must examine and work on. Go forward with all of that understanding and congratulate yourself for being in this moment reading these words.*

- *Remember that we all are, rightfully so, very diverse in so many ways. As you commence down this path of bringing yourself to where you want to be emotionally and in every other way, don't compare yourself to others. You are unique and your life is also unique; no-one else has experienced the life you have lived thus far.*

- *Work towards having, at will, a meditative and reflective mindset available to you. Such a mindset could bring you a new outlook together with a clear resolution. A resolution that you could see yourself achieving, building on and enjoying.*

- *Practise such positive thinking and it could lead you towards new ways of thinking and or meditating. Shy away from fearing failure, think of when you effectively achieved even the smallest goal, believe in yourself.*

- *Know that you are strong and able. Believe that you will survive and flourish.*

- *Every day consider, with gratitude, your fortitude. Be prepared to walk forward.*

- *Believe that you will benefit from your capacity to plan and build a store of gratitude for greater awareness of yourself and your aims.*

- *Remember, only take from this work what you want and only if it sits well with you.*

- *Make every attempt to focus on an internal undercurrent of peace and joy. Actively choose and concentrate on positive thoughts. Don't compare yourself to others and thereby mistakenly allow yourself to dampen your forward-looking thinking.*

- *Reflect upon and choose to love your life going forward. Love yourself and all that you are and as you become all you want to be. Be compassionate and strong each day.*

- *Release yourself from the binds of the past where you were stuck in pain and grief, let go and strive to continuously rejoice in becoming.*

- *In all of the above you are adding to your internal toolbox of skills. In doing so, you are gathering your personal psychological wealth and your own deep satisfaction, and, importantly, developing further goal-setting.*

CHAPTER 1

Letting Go

I understood that I needed to let go of what I had dreamed of; that is, long and loving shared lives with my son Luke and grandson, James. I needed to comprehend and believe that this day, this present moment, was going to be different from those dreams. A world which would never be anywhere near a model of happiness unless I chose to respond differently to events occurring in my existing world. Not the former or the future world, but now in the present moment. I needed to consider each moment of each day when I took a breath for life and love and then to conjure up enough imagination and knowledge to discover the way forward. And that way forward, as I saw it, was to live in the world as it was, rather than lapsing into what might have been, could have been, but never would be. I aimed to live with thoughtful intention. I strived for freedom and independence from the bonds of sadness, despair, or any other harmful emotions and thoughts. I focussed on making every effort to do so and gained more insight as I went forward.

I needed to swing around my early adult life experiences and come to agree and understand the loss of two very important people in my life: my only son and later his only son. Losing them crushed my wellbeing in so many ways. My psychological, physical and mental health took a beating. I have worked hard for many years to be the person I wanted to be as I continued to adopt positivism and resilience as a starting point to live each day.

I still try to practise a new positive behaviour almost every day. In doing so, I also seek and practise new positive strategies to strengthen and continue to build ongoing wellbeing. I do the following things to learn more about how to strengthen and build wellbeing; and, importantly, what not to do!

I have and continue to read books, academic papers, journals, fiction and biographies. I watch television documentaries which speak of people's struggles to regain themselves following trauma. I have watched related movies, skits, self-improvement strategies for health, weight, beauty and other fleeting ideals. Some, if not most, suggest that a reader, like me, should be healthier, skinnier, more elegant and better looking. The following 'ways to success' as above, seem to suggest that a person should be better than others. Those were and are not the ways to success that I have adopted.

So, to explain further, I understood, from the above, that to achieve 'success,' I needed to be quicker, cleverer, younger, better looking and always seeking perfection. Perhaps I needed to be wealthier, or maybe I should have created a litany of wonderful attainments. This was not my dream nor my goal; my choice of end result was not the 'better-than' described accomplishments above. It brought to mind a truism – when enough is not enough, more is never enough. I did not believe that I actually lacked anything except peace of mind. I did not really need to be any of the above 'better than (s)'.

Many willingly pursue the above goals and may be trying to meet the seemingly natural desire to do their best in as many aspects of life as possible. I do not believe it is true that most people set out to fail or to create a lesser self. Like me, many might draw from hard-earnt early and growing personal tool kits to do the very best they can at a time of unbelievable loss and grief, a grey clouded reflection of chaos and terror. Although I came to realise that was, maybe, what I called a way forward. And as I crept forward towards my pathway, I absolutely also knew that I could not dissolve in self-pity because, simply said, that would not assist me. Once I had swallowed that cold, hard truth, I also understood that moving forward was the only alternative to being 'stuck' forever in sadness and loss.

Nonetheless, moving forward and making my own unique life-enhancing and positive choices was a (hard-fought) task for me. Usually in such battles people succeed, or lose, or call it quits too soon when venturing down tracks of trial and error. Some may meet such pursuits with grace, negotiating internally to make a smooth transition from war to peace, or just give up and go home. Identifying the desired outcome, which is to be making one's own life-enhancing and positive choices, before embarking on the journey forward, is perhaps the key for many to continue advancing until that described desired outcome has been achieved.

Many, like you and me, are looking for a purposeful life, with love, contentment and happiness. I know that life gives no love, health or wealth guarantees; these things are not a given. You and I need to love and care for ourselves in order to enjoy love, foster sound health, and have sufficient where-withal to survive any tragedy. And, like a rotating top, the opportunity to make positive choices from one's idiosyncratic truths returns again and again throughout our lives. I know this now and I am in it for the long haul, working towards gaining the lifelong benefits of happiness.

So, this book has two purposes knitted together. The first purpose was and is to share how I overcame fear, overwhelming grief, depression and anger. The second purpose is to share with you how I have broken free from what could have easily become my personal default-setting to trauma.

I should point out though, that for many of the years between the sudden deaths of Luke and James, life gradually returned to everyday 'normal' happiness. For me, normal happiness was still a relative concept. I believe that following the first period of grief, that is, following Luke's death, my efforts to foster new coping skills may have been useful to help me cope with more grace and ease after my grandson James' death. Luke died in 2007 and James died in 2018. What is very clear to me, however, is that the emotional turmoil of trauma and grief I had experienced prior to and following those losses, briefly resurfaced at times. I remain grateful that those grieving times slowly, but not always surely, diverted to strength and confidence as time went on.

Nevertheless, even though I slowly accepted, intellectually and emotionally, the information of each death, I was insistently and unremittingly confronted by the deadly facts. I was shattered, disbelieving, frantic, afraid, lost and at risk of unravelling permanently. I felt primitive anguish, flash by flash, shove by shove, into a colossal hell hole of emotional and physical agony from which there was no escape or release except through utter exhaustion and then fitful sleep. I urgently needed to work on internal and external conduits to recovery. Substantial mental and physical strengths were required, built and gradually set in place.

I have since crossed a bridge; accepting that what was gone was indeed gone. Over significant time I learnt to treasure each day without focussing on or continuously wallowing in self-pity, anger, sadness or loss of good humour. However, that peace of mind was slowly gained at the end of a long hard road; problematic and agonising but nevertheless stubbornly travelled. But take heart dear reader, from my present view that now, a little more each day, I find I love the freedom of being self-directed, the freedom of clarity of thought and purpose and the precious freedom of positivism and constant resilience.

I also believe that, like myself, you too might be happy, without being hurt or made to suffer by others or yourself. I chose not to run any race for instant perfection or to be

13

'better than'. And conversely, for one who believes that happiness is a gift worth working towards, the purpose for myself was and is to always protect and grow my own gift of life happiness, life health and contentment. The happiness-gift is not randomly acquired, but it is possible to earn by my and your hard work.

Therefore, in order to describe how my earlier life had impacted my wellbeing, I have included, in the next chapter, some autobiographical information which is important to this story. Those personal, and for me life-changing, tragic, horrendous and unhappy wretched events were true, immediate and important to my life, then, and now.

- *Be compassionate with yourself, hold an empathic and kind frame of mind throughout your struggles.*

- *Remind yourself that you did not choose your own or another's calamitous life events. If you consider you did contribute towards your unhappy state of being, be strong and proud as you work towards relinquishing all doubt about your present preparedness to grow forward in mind and body. Be patient and continue to become your strong and valuable self.*

- *Tell yourself every day that you are in the process of starting to build your own collection of strategies and tactics. Practise and develop positivity skills for living in each moment. Practise and develop positivism and the letting go of pain a little more each day.*

- *Purposefully generate strong and deep compassion for yourself. Be firm and resolute.*

- *Pick yourself up and learn and determine for yourself what it is that you want from, and for, your life. Write a list!*

- *Care for your wellbeing, focus on growing your positivity and elasticity of thoughts and behaviours. Remind yourself each and every day that you are worth the work and the love.*

- *Practise not endlessly wishing for what you know is not possible, be strong. Practise not dramatically exaggerating and do not allow yourself to whirl out of control. Continue to build your collection of plans and skills for your toolbox and for your future. Practise walking forward into your future.*

CHAPTER 2

Moving Along

A fter many years of work, I now have both personal and professional experience from which to draw, and to strengthen my, and possibly your resolve in achieving life happiness goals. Prior to that work, which continued down a long winding road, I was hoping, trying, struggling and working so very hard to gain confidence and belief in myself. I made a conscious choice to focus on my recovery from trauma. I learned to trust myself in making positive and considered choices, thereby contributing to my mind-peace recovery.

I found making those types of choices could help me to identify what might usefully be done to become the contented person I wished to be. I realised that contentment would encourage making sound choices for going forward. I am committed to self-motivated personal growth; it continues to encourage me.

On this journey I realised that it is helpful to practise methods which positively impact my mind. This was in direct contrast to living in extreme distress.

To repeatedly undertake those positive strategies, is likely to continue and to be of great benefit to my emotional and psychological wellbeing.

When I started on the journey to recovery, I delved into slowly acquiring strong purpose to practise self-discipline as I prepared to find clear and strong paths towards happiness. I used the brick-by-brick steps I had become accustomed to adopting. I welcomed and risked a self-adjustment in thinking while also gradually and thankfully increasing my self-respect and self-esteem. I appreciate my present wellbeing.

Throughout this book you might wonder why I revisit the past throughout and speak of the present and the future, in a back-and-forth way. Life in general, I speculate, is not always a smooth transition from babyhood to childhood, or through adolescence to adult life.

And this is why, at each step of the way, both you and I are likely to stop and reflect, we might try another approach and move backwards and forwards with our ideas, decisions and learning. And I believe each of these chapters takes a different approach to all of my life experiences and how I dealt with them. So, I do indeed slide backwards and forwards throughout. Each new scenario for me is exactly that — a new challenge which requires a different view and a different approach to everything that has gone before.

I have learnt to persistently treasure each day and try to live each moment of the day without self-pity, anger, sadness or loss of good humour. You too might take up that challenge. But, for me, that slowly flowering peace of mind was elusive.

It came at the end of a long rocky way, hard and agonising but nevertheless, stubbornly travelled. Now I find I love the freedom of being self-directed. I increasingly benefit from clarity of thought and purpose. I enjoy the precious freedom of positivism and constant resilience. I do not deny myself anything true, positive and safe that might contribute towards working towards daily happiness.

Sound challenging? It was and is, but throughout the ongoing chapters I describe my confronting experiences and ways forward. I offer strategies, approaches, various tactics and further ways forward in order to achieve lifelong goals of living in the moment each and every day.

For example, one strategy I have utilised over time is to simply use my self-determination. Determination was crucial for me to achieve acceptance of what was. What a fight! Acceptance to put aside unending grief, yet striving to embrace compassion for myself, watching the meanderings of my mind as I wished for the return of my boys, and wishing for a different outcome. I dreamed they would walk through the door again and allow me to love and enjoy them for the rest of my life. And of course, that fantasy never eventuated. I had to accept that it would never happen. Acceptance was critical to moving forward.

But, following smidgens of dawning acceptance, I discovered that the ensuing tactics of mental self-examination, self-actualising processes and determined progress towards happiness were set within the context of my pain, loss and conflicted thoughts. I have now, after much of the aforesaid hard work and a gentle easing in my mind of the terrible loss of both of my boys, stepped forward to welcome the unknown in order to make life-affirming positive choices.

I now actually delight in choosing emotional positivity and resilience over sadness, anger, or self-pity. These choices seem to be so much more beneficial rather than endlessly dithering about whether or not to 'do it, say it, write it, or live it'. I am, for the most part, contented with how I am living my life and have very few, if any, regrets apart from understanding that I will always be regretful for the loss of my boys. I also understand that I can regret their loss of life forever, knowing that nothing can change the facts. But it is my choice and privilege to live with this sorrow in parallel to choosing to love life and enjoy it to the fullest.

At present I mostly describe myself as a resilient and happy optimist. Except for when I am not, or perhaps, when I am mentally responding to a perception that my rights to hold my loved ones for as long as *I live*, have been dispensed with by circumstances beyond anyone's absolute control. I then think of the poem by Reinhold Niebuhr about having the courage to accept what cannot be changed and also having the wisdom to know the difference. The difference, that is, between what cannot be changed and what might be changed. I strove and continue to strive for such wisdom.

But earlier, as I reflect back, I recall that as a child I was told I was wilful. I guess to some extent I was perhaps a little determined even then. However, I celebrated what others might have perceived to be a shortcoming in my character, because that so-called wilfulness has spurred me on to explore my choices. I stumbled upon finding I have some talent, boosted by many hours of hard work, for study, academic writing, coaching, exploring and assessment and therapeutic counselling. I continue to try and focus my energies on meaningful, sustaining and agreeable work as I recognise that such work is positivism in action.

Nevertheless, each of us could likely describe negative conditions or experiences, like stress, trauma, grief, or mental illness in different and individualistic terms. And of course, each of us is an individual situated in our own personal and different circumstances. One size does not fit all! Each of us has the opportunity, if we explore our options with courage, to experience what we consider our greatest stress. It is our choice how we deal with it. Awareness and adjustment of my or your reactions to that stress are critically important in the journey forward. Our thoughts and behaviours too, must be directed towards positive goals, such as daily enjoyment and life-long happiness.

- *Ask yourself – what is it that I really want? What are my priorities? – are they my happiness, my partner and or children, my career, or my mental and physical health? Write yourself a list, double check your specific goals, try to prioritise what is most important to you.*

- *Then, determine and utilise your strategies around what it is that you really want. Work on pinpointing your goals and build them into your cache of strengths and personal skills. Write yourself a list of what to do!*

- *Rework all of the above every day in order to achieve focus and your chosen outcomes. Write yourself a list of what strategies work best for you. Utilise those as important ways forward.*

- *Improve your positive thought processes in order to work stronger, bolder and with never- flagging gratitude for your life and all wonderful ensuing opportunities.*

- *Know that you are, in every moment, working towards your rich and desired life; love your loved ones even more and let them know how you feel as you delight in their company in every moment*

- *Let go of all fractious people who would pull you down. Encourage and cultivate yourself as you develop your strategies and toolbox.*

- *Focus on your purpose, energise each day and enrich yourself with hope and with your hard work. Take care of and greatly value your body, mind and good health.*

CHAPTER 3

Early Days

When I was quite young, I had no post-high school education and very little life experience outside of my home life. At home I had my mother and father, three brothers and two sisters. As a teenager I had a boyfriend who would later become my first husband. As I look back, I know we siblings enjoyed our respective childhoods although, of course, we each had a different perspective of how our lives were travelling.

We siblings are all about two years or so apart. And our experiences of our parents, as they themselves matured and aged, seemed to have been rather different. Each of us had quite dissimilar experiences of our parents as they and we matured.

For example, one of us might have asked the other "Do you remember when . . .?" At times we could each relate times when we saw things through different eyes, some younger and some older. Looking back, it now seems like a microscopic description of the world; all individuals seeing things from different perspectives, ages, backgrounds and impressions from our early and later family lives. Notwithstanding such divergent views and experiences of each other and our late parents, we all now continue to enjoy each other's company, partners, in-laws, nieces, nephews and of course, every wonderful child.

Married when I was a teenager, (my mother told me I was too young but I knew better!), I soon found that the person I married struggled to maintain a peaceful composure.

However, when I was twenty-two, he and I had our only child, a beautiful son. Unfortunately for me, the illusion of a loving couple's life dissolved under very difficult and extreme circumstances. I made a decision to leave the marriage and moved house with my infant child Luke. Following the move, I had very little money, only that which I had borrowed from my not-well-off but generous parents. I look back now in awe at how I coped during that time. Being financially desperate, I returned to the former marital home after about a week to retrieve some of Luke's clothes, toys and equipment.

At the house I was disappointed but not surprised to find all of the locks changed. There were men up on the roof of a nearby higher building site who watched me trying to get in. One asked if I needed some help. I responded truthfully by saying I did not seem to have the right keys.

He came over with his workmate who brought a ladder. He cheerfully went onto the roof, took off some tiles, entered the house and then let me in. When I had quickly placed the essentials into my borrowed car, I relocked the door from the inside and left as soon as I could. I found that when you have nothing, necessity makes courage critical.

My little one and I lived near my parents. Luke later went to kindergarten and I then completed a child development course at university. I didn't know at the time that this tentative step in reaching out to the world to seek a new life, in order to create better means for myself and Luke, would be the genesis of many new experiences in my life. I worked persistently in various part-time employment opportunities. Later I completed a bachelor's degree with first-class Honours. I was then academically comfortable enough to apply for an Australian Commonwealth Scholarship with the hopes of being funded to finish a further four years of study for my doctorate. I won the gift of a scholarship and achieved a PhD in the Health and Social sciences. I will always be very grateful for those opportunities.

Now after many years in various fields of human service work, I continue to work, with great enjoyment, in a private capacity as a Life Happiness Coach, mediator, counsellor and author. I write because it interests me and I love writing. It also allows me to talk to myself and reflect on my previous and ensuing experiences in life.

However, at the time when I separated from my child's father, my life had a way of changing so quickly that at times I felt like I was a spinning top. I divorced, bought a little house, enrolled at university and cared for my child. Four or five years later I met my now-husband, Peter. He brought into the mix his little daughter Georgia who now has an adult child, Alex, with her former partner David.

Then, years later, my life pathway changed forever. One very late night, Peter and I received a call from one of Luke's friends who quickly told us that he thought Luke was dying. Luke had been attacked by a group of three, or possibly four, substance-affected people. (The Court did not determine that there was a fourth person even though there was a suggestion made in the Court that there was a fourth perpetrator.)

When we arrived, we found we were too late; our son had died from his extensive injuries. Our grandson, James, then aged about seven or eight years, had thankfully been sleeping in his bedroom throughout the terrible assault upon his father that took place outside their home.

We gathered James up and took him home with us. Therefore, from that point on, our grieving process was interrupted and influenced by the very real and important emotional and psychological needs of our grandchild. We struggled for some time in absolute grief, always juggling that grief with the attentive care we wanted to give James. I am not quite sure now how we managed those processes but we did manage to place James at the forefront of our attention during those terrible days and for weeks and months following. We also managed to let go of thoughts about the perpetrators, the trial and the ensuing outcomes for each of those people.

My strategies for survival and for ongoing life-happiness had begun to coalesce. I determined to carry out essential responsibilities each day. We each chose the other as our primary support. I also had the wonderful benefit of speaking, for quite some time with dear colleagues, who offered me time and patience to pour out my grief. Their counsel was invaluable as was my medical practitioner's very welcome time and counsel. Family and friends could not do enough for me and Peter.

Peter and I walked and talked and listened to each other as we shared our concerns with each other. We also took care to ensure freely-given demonstrations of our respect were given for the other's daily changing attitudes, demeanours and states of mind.

We gently reminded ourselves that, notwithstanding our grief, neither one of us or any other person, or deity, could change anything that had happened that dreadful night.

We bought James what he needed and commenced introducing various activities to him. We gave James the time and structure he needed and ensured we kept up with his changing attitudes, demeanours and state of mind.

I worked like there was no tomorrow for fear of languishing in grief. I took leave from formal employment and instead cared for James, cleaned, gardened, washed, cooked and counselled myself endlessly.

I reminded myself that I understood, (and continue to understand) that the ideals of equity, fairness and justice are just that: ideals. I talked to myself frequently about wishes being just that, wishes. They were and are not realities and not freely dispersed according to some numerical or star chart calculation. I needed to move forward and I needed to believe that I was strong enough to fail in some way every day and still keep moving. I made every effort to undertake all manner of risks. Not dangerous risks but simply being prepared to examine my way forward and to be prepared to walk in another direction if necessary.

Times were tough and I required effort and strength to move forward each day in some way. I knew I would be mistaken not to strive for life going forward. I needed to live and value my life. Grief, particularly pervasive grief, was exhausting. It consumed vast amounts of my energy. Grief seemed determined to wait in the wings for its moment of release. I endeavoured to be compassionate with myself and I didn't press myself to do any particular thing during those stages. However, at the end of every day, there was simply no getting away from the fact that any time is the right time to value life and to work forward as much as possible.

The first few weeks after Luke's death were unbelievably difficult. Apart from the total unbelievability of him being killed and the mirror image of the actual fact of his death, I think I may have entered into a dream-like state as I waited for myself to enter into reality once again. And of course, I did return to being a more thinking, rather than grieving person, because of my responsibilities and because of the rapid onset of other challenges; an important one was to arrange Luke's funeral.

Then, three weeks following Luke's death, my sister-in-law Julie suicided. Our entire extended family seemed numb and my brother was so very shocked and traumatised. He had, just three weeks previously, lovingly and carefully built the funeral flower display for Luke's funeral. We each considered that Luke's death had possibly impacted Julie in ways that we might never recognise. Once again grief, like any other emotion, needed release.

Looking back now, I can see that it was and is possible to run with grief in a healthy way while at the same time caring for oneself and to give love and support to others. Giving to others is a wonderfully healing thing. I realised this, for example, when I spoke at Julie's funeral which I simply could not do at Luke's funeral. It was so very important for me to try to lift my brother up from his depths of despair and I made every effort to do so, as did the entire family, as they had done for me, Peter and James. In the midst of these disastrous times, I again came to understand that I needed to gather inner strength so as not to fall into chaotic, stressed, or endless sadness. I knew I would never give up my memories but neither would I give up my determination to find a strong impetus to move forward.

Peter and I have worked hard to pull ourselves back together again. It was difficult work but each of us believed and continue to believe that our capacities to choose life and happiness instead of grief and hopelessness have allowed us to regain our former selves. I love life and I love my memories of my dear son Luke and, of course, beloved James. I stay in touch with Layla, my late son's now adult daughter who lives in the country.

I live life to the fullest, it is the only life I will have and sharing it with Peter is a legacy beyond measure. Our relationship has been a treasured gift, a loving journey which I continue to share with you all.

- *Important strategies: As far as you can, allow your grief to subside, let go of anger at yourself or others, never allow yourself to have anger rule your mood or actions, do not become immobilised by anger; you have too much to lose. Instead build and protect your inner strength as you heal from within.*

- *Talk to trusted people who you believe will listen without criticism or impatience, but who will help and guide you.*

- *Remind yourself that this is the only life you have; forgive and love yourself as the unique human being that you are and determine to take a valuable and responsible role in your unique life.*

- *Seek out and discover what brings you peace even if it is, in the beginning, only for a short time. Inner tranquillity is a foundation for your peaceful mindset, your internal security, and your belief and confidence in yourself.*

- *Make every effort to doggedly believe you will recover, start to look forward to learning and discovering new and exciting pathways towards happiness. Believe in your choice to be a person who can think for yourself with free will and self-love.*

- *Try to work towards acceptance of what is.*

- *Acceptance is really simply the opposite of fighting and disbelieving absolute reality wherein you sink into anxiety, constantly being upset and anguished.*

- *Acceptance points to a less anxious mind and towards the possible growth of a peaceful mind. Work on your acceptance of what is!*

- *You will become more focussed and ready to embrace growing forward into happiness. As you develop acceptance of what is, you will be accomplishing small steps towards being part of the peaceful resolve of every day and less of the stress you may be experiencing.*

Chapter 4

Reaching Forward

As described earlier, my life experiences had seriously impacted my wellbeing and fuelled a purposeful and personal search for happiness. Life experience has directed my pathways and sent me towards seeking resolute fulfilment. My adult working-life background, coupled together with my experience as a social scientist, dispute resolution practitioner/therapist/and mediator has provided me with a certain set of skills. I use those skills daily in assisting myself and others to resolve issues and dilemmas.

The above work has, for the most part, enabled switching on light-globe-clarification of my own and other people's focussed decision making. Particularly when I and they have not known, initially, which way to go in life. Decision making in relation to attempted suicides, in acutely antagonistic parental divorce wars, or a simple dilemma of choosing the next step or, even when struggling to decide to stay without change. The counselling, assessing and mediating has also included perspectives and recommendations towards children's best interests.

Throughout the following chapters I describe situations in which I and others have suffered setbacks, and how I have had the privilege of assisting some of those people. However, this book mainly focusses on my story and how I endeavour to compassionately and lovingly describe strategies and tactics to perhaps assist you to achieve your goals of happiness.

You undoubtedly would know other individuals, perhaps friends, relations, neighbours, and others, who all describe widely-differing views of their personal and sometimes tragic situations. Many reflect on similar grief, loss and pain as my own personal and heart-breaking life experiences. My travels throughout life have provided me with many insights into my psyche and wellbeing as well as into other peoples' lives and wellbeing. I am always amazed at the myriad of ways in which any one person might react to different dilemmas or complex situations.

And so, I have also discovered that I am now, every day, grateful for the opportunities I have been given. I am grateful for being capable of focussing on becoming positivity-conscious and determined enough to make life choices through which I achieve goals for happiness. These opportunities continue at times to assist me to help others resolve issues which have hampered their pathways forward to happiness.

The above-described work, which I continue to enjoy as a life happiness coach, has been challenging, worthwhile and valuable. Worthwhile for myself and worthwhile for the people I have always sought to serve with critical insight, kindness and compassion.

As previously explained though, the roads forward have been challenging, scary at times or simply perceived to be too hard. There seemed to be so many roadblocks along the way, ones that needed surmounting, by sliding along, or pushing them aside and continuously making attempts to live with purpose and steadfast intent.

So, do any of the following seem to obstruct your road forward? Over time I faced and dealt with each of these blocks in relation to myself. I was blocked when I failed to accept what has twice been and gone. I could not let it go. I was blocked when, each time, I could not believe what had happened and I could not believe my boys' and my misfortune. The gravity of my situation reflected the enormity of sudden death and wilful, grievously wrought killing which is akin to tragic situations that we all hear about in the media.

Knowing that others were suffering like me didn't ease my pain or have me give way to grace. I was also blocked for some time as I continued to query whether I always needed to forgive in order to find happiness. At my worst and saddest times, I was blocked when I seemed caught in a place where I considered everyone else wrong, mean, selfish, hateful and controlling.

I stalled when I had issues with self-responsibility: I was unable to do anything except wallow in my grievous pain, notwithstanding I understood I was hindering my own efforts to step forward. And, how did I make the right decisions for myself, how did I choose the most beneficial path for myself?

It took me years – not days, weeks or months, but years

to commence taking down those blocks and start to build brick-by-brick new pathways. I explored and practised meditation, yoga and other mindful activities. I talked with family members each time they would put up with me. I endlessly spoke with, and nearly drove my very forthright, practical, loving husband mad.

I also knew that stress, lack of sleep and endless whys and wherefores were eating away at my physical health. I was becoming tired; I was experiencing endless turmoil and emotional stress and I did not want to go down the road of needing formal mental health treatment. I know what stress, following the loss of a loved one or other tragic circumstances, does to a person's heart health, such as increasing the potential for stroke. This knowledge contributed towards the impetus for me to get up and get going. I also knew in my heart that being physically incapacitated or dying was not my goal and certainly not a way forward to happiness.

Each of us will have experienced a time, at some level I imagine, where choices can be made to allow ourselves either to swing into depression or, conversely, gather strength. With strength, you and I can choose to work towards improved mental and physical resilience. An important secret is to pay highly selective attention to bringing your consciousness and energy purposefully into yourself.

I decided that my purpose would focus on discovering my specific life comfort/happiness goals. In those ways I commenced to discover, celebrate and enjoy happiness and joy for myself and those I love. I wrote out an ever-changing list. I formed a multitude of strategies and approaches in order to reach self-acceptance, self-forgiveness for existing and for not achieving instant success. I worked towards taking responsibility for decision-making. I examined ways, as I still do, wherein I try insistently to bolster my personal happiness growth through my everyday focus and self-work.

My words and my story, as told throughout this book, have helped me to continue to re-examine my choices and I now seek further opportunities for growth and self-awareness. To provide me with strategic ways wherein I might improve my outlook, wellbeing, mindset, and capacity to examine my own crucial decision-making about my life pathways, expectations, and hopes for lifelong happiness.

- *Focus on how you might positively deal with and manage your experiences.*

- *We are the sum of our life experiences and that reveals we are also the sum of how we deal with and manage those experiences.*

- *Consider and reflect on the ways you have dealt with your life experiences.*

- *For example, you may want to make difficult or focussed decisions but resist the effort and resist expending the energy. Now, in this present moment, is your time to make the effort and expend the energy.*

- *Blocks to your growth and wellbeing occur – of course they will but you get a choice. Try to identify your own specific blocks to progress, make your own list of blocks and list some ideas about how you might challenge and overcome those hindrances. Have you been criticised to the point of losing confidence? Have you been condemned for what others have seen as poor behaviour on your part? Have you learned to fight in ways that have only brought you grief and perhaps shame?*

- *Choose to let go of each of the above hindrances, be tolerant and compassionate with yourself. Again, write your list of all you want to deliver for yourself from yourself, seek your own approval, acceptance, love, fairness, appreciation and self-belief. Practise every day reading and writing about those qualities as they relate to you and immerse yourself in love, praise and confidence as you go forward.*

- *Care for yourself and each of your everyday choices; carefully evaluate each one so that you can be purposeful in your forward thinking and actions.*

CHAPTER 5

A Heart-to-Heart Special

....

D o you think you would like to be regarded with kindness, courtesy, equality, respect and hopefully, love? I speculate that might be true for many of us. Sometimes you might have been afraid of, or been threatened by taking the initiative in life. Think of trying to go into the sea when you imagined it would be cold and forbidding. You then poked a toe in and it wasn't too bad! You actually took the first, then second, then third step into the sea. You remember being encouraged by your parents and playmates. But you were the person who took the plunge and you faced the challenge.

Venturing forth socially is something you can now do, in the same way as you learnt to go into the sea or go to school on the first day. And what if you are not always treated with the above qualities of kindness, courtesy and so on? Not all people respond as we might like. Depending on the setting, we can choose to stay or leave, or greet everyone with good cheer, or be reserved and wait until you seem to have found a likeminded person to speak with.

We know that whoever and wherever we are, human interactions at times appear to be quite confusingly diverse. Perhaps such awkwardness is not easily woven into the threads of our intimate worlds. Remember, you are likely to choose the people with whom you would like to be in a relationship. You are able to decide with whom you are friendly or intimate with and so on.

You might ask yourself how you like your current relationships. Are they as satisfying, mutually rewarding, respectful and as loving as you wish them to be? How can you work towards enjoying relationships with the important people in your world? Are you content with the friendships you share with others? I recall my former self being afraid and living with crushing disappointment in those I thought cared for me. Was I now making the 'right' decisions for me? How can you decide what is the 'right' decision for you? You can determine and choose not to live with fear, you can choose to protect and respect your choices.

It seems evident that some relationships have toxic outcomes wherein one person or the other might be left with longstanding trauma, even to the extent of post-traumatic stress disorder or other disabling anxieties. My ideas about my self-worth were almost, previously, completely shattered. I lost confidence, felt unloved, unaccepted, lost, and unhappy. I lived in pain and thought that perhaps I would never find happiness with a kind and loving person. I had come to doubt my decision-making.

If you are in a precarious situation and are experiencing

violence or other trauma you may find it difficult to decide what to do. It is important to recognise that some people use verbal denigrating abuse, mental manipulation of others, physical or sexual abuse, child abuse, financial or simple authoritarian abuse to gain a measure of control over others. A difficult person might present many faces. I have worked with people who clearly offered histories of a disordered early life. Some of those people might have learnt to survive by shunning intimacy or gentleness and might have yearned for, but never found, what they have sought.

Such a person might not have learnt how to love or how to find acceptance.

How might this sad, angry, possibly dangerous person succeed in transforming earlier experiences into a positive present life? If you are with such a person, and he or she has refused professional mental health treatment or behaviour-adjusting assistance, you must make a decision. You should make self-protective and strong choices about your strategic life pathways.

Consideration of our life journeys is so important to our life happiness. You and I should not believe we do not have authority or choices.

As I reflect upon my earlier life, I understand that I was very young. I also then believed I had no authority. At that time, I did not believe things could be different than they unhappily were. I perceived that my child's father and I held different ways of looking at the world and had very little in common. Friendly, open discussions were not part of the relationship. I finally understood that I was to some extent responsible for this state of affairs, because, by my apparent acceptance of those differing views, I was seemingly giving permission to the other person to carry on regardless.

I learnt through experience to understand that my previous manner of thinking had led me to believe I was the sad person I had become because I had consistently thought I had no authority. I also believed external influences were responsible for my dilemma and that I faced complex challenges and insurmountable problems.

I talked to friendly people I trusted... I didn't really want to ask them what I should do, partly to avoid revealing my predicament. It was quite a dilemma; separation and divorce were not on my family of origin's agenda, or on mine at that time. I was so frightened of the future that I was at my wit's end as to know what I should do. I chose instead to talk and listen to people about what they were doing with their lives. I loved listening to people talk about what they anticipated happening with their relationships, what they would like to achieve in life and what they did to make themselves happy and, importantly for me, what motivated them. I gained much from all of that talking and still do.

I practised with the early tools I used for healing: meditation and most importantly, living in the moment rather than reflecting on the past. The calm meditation gave me clarity and perspective. I was able to do much needed soul-searching to start a journey of insight and understanding. Again, this was really hard work. Throughout, even though many of the events around my life were challenging, I could see with ever-increasing clarity that I had a choice in how I let my responses determine my life as the future unfolded.

I was also motivated to try another strategy which was to do something just for me. I wrote lists about what I could do to ease my pain and how to get to a more peaceful place. I agreed with myself that nothing was going to occur over-night and I accepted that my determination might wear a bit thin over time. I am grateful thus far that my determination may have been shaky at times but it has not worn too thin. I found that I needed to walk quite a few diverse pathways looking for confidence, peace and contentment. I needed to anticipate different and or new decision making and I kept the faith; faith in myself and my willingness and perseverance to keep on fighting. I also knew that I would sometimes come to the end of a path without discovering anything that I had wanted to discover. But that was okay, I knew instant success was not going to happen as much as I knew that I would, absolutely would, get better and better at finding my own valuable ways forward.

I later grew enough to take charge and become aware of the need to give myself permission to have personal author-ity, to take control of my own feelings and to find other points of view. My life direction needed impetus for change. I also looked outwards for my wellbeing. I had reached a turnaround in my journey. The turn was comprised of self-control and self-authority; it led me to be more effective in my independence and life decisions. I enjoyed and still enjoy looking forward every day to enriching my wide-ranging relationships, from the personal to the professional.

I found there are many ways of relating to the people in my world including the above-described ways. The important people in my present world include Peter my husband, all close family members, casual and long-term friends and extended family members.

I have good and enjoyable relationships with my stepdaughter, and step-grandson, my brothers, sisters, their children, the in-laws, cousins, childhood friends; I have more recently-gained friends and many dear colleagues. I have fleeting or long-term relationships with neighbours and various government departments with whom I must interact at times. I have had a child and a grandson and I have a granddaughter.

In some circumstances, families might, or might not promote independence. Some families might not encourage loved ones to look for freedom from 'what-always-went-before' or 'this-is-the-way-we-have-always-done-it'. Family culture can limit one's views. I understand and accept that most young people today, just like yesterday, work towards living their own lives. They, like you and me, make their own circumstances fit their needs as they choose. I celebrate those persons as they engage in taking responsibility for their own lives and pathways.

As I improved my relationship with myself and by extension my relationships with others, I let go of criticising and judging myself and others. I previously decided I now had a choice in decision- making, and I took time to flex this 'have a choice' idea around in my head. I believe that I, and each of you might, and can, courageously choose to take personal responsibility in decision-making and life choices.

Taking care of and being responsible for my health and wellbeing were also essential factors in taking care of my own progress towards to life happiness; these are critically-important choices for your life happiness as well. I had to ask myself how long I would allow myself to live in fear, or to wallow in self-pity, or to clutch at a nonsense question about whether or not I could move on. When I presented these questions to myself, clarity of purpose arrived faster than previously. Hence, I was free to reject the self-torture those negative emotions caused. So, by coming to this decision, I gave myself permission to help myself. This was an important key for me to heal faster that even professional help could not achieve. You too can use this key to heal and grow into happiness. I decided to take responsibility for my thoughts, and for my mental and physical health, and my food and alcohol intake, including both the quality and quantity of my food and alcohol intake. Initially you might find taking such personal responsibility a little frightening. However, many of us are blessed with an abundance of food options, however not all promote healthy outcomes. I still mindfully focus on consuming a minimal amount of meat, as well as more fresh vegetables and fruit. I choose the people with whom I want to spend time. I outgrow some relationships and further develop others. This is an important thread for you to develop in order to step forward into your desired life.

Friends and relatives seek my time and company at times as I do theirs similarly to what you may experience. The people I want to bring closer are those I love, care for and admire, the ones who bring positive attitudes, value, contentment and fulfilment to the relationship. I believe that positivity, resilience and joyful wellbeing are ways in which I can set myself free from negativity which I know can only attack and damage my wellbeing and encourage unhappiness. You too can choose your close companions; the ones upon whom you might rely to help you grow your positivity, resilience and joyful wellbeing.

I choose to work towards looking forward to being content, picking my own course and making my own decisions, both big and little. I can now demonstrate to myself and those who would have me do 'it' their way, that I have pride in myself. I know and demonstrate that I believe myself to be a valuable person with significant worth.

Please don't be fooled into thinking any of this was an easy road! It was not! I did not want to live separately and alone. I did not want to have narrow and compulsive tunnel vision. I wanted my relationships with others to build my and their well-being. I wanted so much! I wanted independence and happiness in going forward into myself by being contented and braver each day. And I found and continue to find myself becoming more confident as I relate my thoughts and behaviours to people who are close to me and to the world at large. I no longer choose to be a finished or limited by-product as in 'this is who I am and I cannot change and cannot do what

I want'. This state of reasoning/being occurred gradually and allowed me to believe my life to be self-fulfilling and not predetermined. I gradually reversed my previous inclination for self-defeating repetitious refusals to believe I could make changes in any facet of my life. I now love this track and I sometimes become quite excited at what I have achieved.

I consider that genuine friendships allow you and me to agree with another person's interest in striving for close loving relationships. If love is a central part of any relationship, either the lover or the loved, each would likely express their changing perspectives, thoughts, needs and directions. Each person permitting the other to be what they wish. Is this achievable? Why not? I, like many others, was previously under the mistaken impression that one person in a relationship *was* more powerful and therefore more rightfully set in his or her ways than the other (me). Therefore, this impression persuaded me (as I believed then I was the less powerful person) that I should submit to the other's will.

However, I knew that choices could and must be made if I wished to live with loving respectful mutuality and everyday contentment. I worked hard to change my thoughts about sorrow and anguish, loss and perceived power. There was a period, prior to breaking free from the past, where I came to believe that if I had to remain the same ineffective person, it was certainly not my fault, it was the fault of the other. I am grateful that I was determined enough to work through with strategies to improve my lot.

A budding acorn of realisation paved the way for change.

I realised that my more mindful responses and the actions that followed could be of my choosing. I started to appreciate that my inner and actual world may not always have been as I wished and I began developing personal control regarding how I dealt with what Life presented me.

I tried to practise 'fake it until I make it' strategies. I wittingly employed hope instructively and still do. As often as I could I practised self-confidence. It sounds strange doesn't it, to 'practise' confidence. However, I persevered with these strategies until I succeeded in reflecting my realities with a sense of self control and pride in working towards a happier self. I worked towards being powerful when it came to shaping my own realities, until my work for self-belief predicated giving up the 'fake it' and evolved into clear and unequivocal 'make it'.

I, like most people, including you, dear reader, want to be my own authority and director. I believe now that I am the real deal with hope, positivism and resilience. I also know that external authority is demonstrated in life everywhere. This becomes clear when I try to argue with the local council, or someone who doesn't believe inequality exists, or a man who says 'she made me do it' or against higher fees for utilities, a court's verdict, or a police officer wanting to issue a ticket and so on. In a personal relationship though, I would never choose to be (clearly wisely), as you should never choose to be, submissive when confronted with an untrustworthy or unpredictable person.

I make every effort to maintain solidarity with myself

as I look forward to increasingly becoming conscious and reflective of my experiences. You too can make those efforts and benefit from them. All my experiences, the personal, the professional, life-changing tragic events and invaluable friendships make up my life. I value this life, as you might strive to value yours. I am very mindful of those life experiences in the same way that you can be mindful. Over the years I have used them all as relevant keys to changing my thoughts, habits, timid attitudes and behaviours to always be 'becoming' my authentic and contented self. You too, can use your relevant and learnt keys to be always 'becoming' your authentic and contented self.

- *Planning strategies, actions and forward moving thoughts and behaviours are necessary for you to let go of the past.*

- *Let go of those accompanying endless ruminations of what was, what could have been or that which might have been. Contemplate your future happy life instead.*

- *Make a new pact with yourself and break from that ill-fated past. Enter into your brave new beginnings knowing that now you must be the decision-maker about your life happiness. Always acknowledge the past as learnt lessons and trust your inner self.*

- *However, go slowly in trying to achieve your end goals for yourself; instead try to focus on the immediate things you can do, learn and strive for that might be achieved in a reasonable time frame.*

You can manage your time and take small steps, think about the now of each day and pinpoint your focus on building internal personal strength.

- *Resilience, personal growth, optimism and strategic planning all contribute to building positive forward shifts towards life happiness. These are some of your inner qualities which are to be valued and developed further each day.*

- *Or, from a different angle, if you realise, or even if you do not realise, that life is simply the way you find it and the way you act in it and upon it, then life is still indeed, as it is. You can accept that or not. Decision making and choices will frame your views and actions.*

- *Try to remember that acceptance leads to the next step which is to seek movements forward; if acceptance continues to elude you then so will peace and happiness elude you. Be brave, loving and compassionate to yourself each and every day.*

CHAPTER 6

Choosing Happiness

I have briefly described the life-altering moment when my beloved son died. In the weeks that followed, I processed grief while our grandson James, was at school or fast asleep in bed. Even so, I struggled to find a balance between sharing and speaking about my grief and loss with Peter and other family members and being closely aware of James' needs.

So rather than overwhelm James with my grief, I endeavoured to respond sensitively and appropriately to this dear little boy, in order to help him process his own feelings. We also shared and relived the many happy memories James had of his father. He liked to speak of his wonderful memories of him and his father walking in the hills, going camping and his great birthday parties.

Throughout, I worked hard to introduce James to my perspectives regarding being happy, in language that a child could understand. I explained to James as he grew up, how certain challenges required me to start building personal strength of character in order to improve my life. (I believed

I was getting there). I communicated to him that life is about being happy and being committed to gaining skills and strategies. I explained that each person's experiences will generally have led their life to circumstances they might never have guessed would appear.

I have spoken about using my personal experiences to encourage people, a person just like you perhaps, who find themselves in very difficult life situations, to remain steadfast in their beliefs of themselves. I talked generally about how people face many experiences of sadness, danger and so on. Over time and as James grew older, we spoke of his immediate and long-term reactions to the death of his beloved father.

Later, James and I spoke about loss and grief including how he puzzled over the loss of his mother to very difficult circumstances and the loss of his half-siblings to out-of-home-care situations. James knew friends who had lost loved ones through horrific accidents, suicide, or natural causes. He knew a family where more than one member of the family had died tragically. However, for the most part James was a very happy boy.

These were important conversations between James and me, Peter and James' half-siblings and his friends. These are important conversations for each of us. You yourself may share such conversations with more than one member of your family or other people important to you. Or you too could perhaps have experienced times of dire illness, desperate unhappiness, poverty, alcoholism, drug abuse or homelessness. You might be living with or have lived with a violent partner or child or parent; you may have been terrorised perhaps or suffered poor mental health or paralysing depression. I believe you *can* choose to heal. I believe making clear and unequivocal decisions about making one's life meaningful and choosing happiness are very important to each of us.

I have been grateful to be able to find great healing and comfort in our extended families and many loving friends. Another important and key tool which I use in daily practise, is to choose humour and laughter in whatever I face each day. Laughter is and was so very important to me in 'getting there'. I tried not to take my situation too seriously so as not to again fall into sadness. I knew that I could choose to scream with ineffective rage and fall into sorrow and unhappiness. Or I could choose to crack up at some nonsensical aspect of my dilemma. For example, I will always recall the roof-men coming to assist me with getting into my locked house to get some things for James. I was so pleased with the way that dilemma turned out, and I can still laugh with delight every time I think of it!

My choice would actually make my management of the situation work differently for me. I could move forward in laughter, hope and love, or waste myself in gloom and doom as I focussed on the unfairness of loss and living with acceptance of that loss. At one stage I questioned the universe's purpose in choosing me to experience these losses, as in 'why me?'. And then of course I could only answer my question with an equally simple answer 'well, why not me?' A question without any logical or satisfactory answer, just another facet of reality that cannot be wished or washed away, changed or altered.

Some months following my son Luke's death, and as James was becoming settled into his supportive school, I returned to work. I was working in a human service area, assessing people in conflict regarding their children. Subsequently, I was providing written assessments to those who would determine legal outcomes for those conflicted petitioners.

Prior to recommencing work though, I slowly built yet another pattern of thinking forward. I realised that I needed to live, work and act with authenticity as much as I could. It was not that I had acted without authenticity before, but at that time I simply wanted to be my essential self. That is, I wanted to acknowledge and release the depths of my despair. I had a new role and life as a parent/grandparent and it was important to manage and honour that new role and new life.

Even so, I could not evade my feelings, or dismiss the hard questions from family, friends, acquaintances or from myself. These questions flowed from everywhere. For example, my now late mother was concerned for my wellbeing. Friends, neighbours and acquaintances made comments about the difficulties of raising a child who had suffered so much loss. Many people had a lot of advice and many more had too many questions. I stayed as close as I could to living in the moment. Concentrating on this day and these tasks, focussing on every little promising smile from James, reading every one of his beautiful letters to me telling me how much he loved me.

Of course, in the early days there were still times when I needed to comfort and provide solace to myself. I sometimes sat and watched a DVD for comfort. The DVD had been continually running in the funeral chapel during Luke's funeral service. It showed the life of Luke in pictures from when he was a little boy, to when he was a teenager and then as an adult and father. In the early days following his death I would cry incessantly and feel very close to him. Then I would shake myself; and work really hard to take charge, smile and laugh. I determined to have some purposeful and uplifting thoughts over the next few hours. I would look through the photographs of Luke and James fishing and camping; and all of the happy birthday parties James had enjoyed since he was placed into his father's care. It was at this point I started to have a sense of what healthy grieving might look like. The grieving was valid and needed to be experienced and not put aside. However, I also needed to restore and be compassionate towards myself. As I stumbled along this potholed avenue, I tried to extend taking charge of myself for a few more hours, then days, and then a few weeks and so on. After Julie's death three weeks following Luke's death, my brother and I sat and cried over Luke and over Julie. We cried ourselves out and propped each other up. Then we started to slowly understand that was enough of such a high and intense level of grief and stress and perhaps we could find more constructive ways to get ourselves together. We agreed we would try as hard as we could to move on.

I suspect that as a consequence of my trauma and grief, I

was able to draw upon the experiences of my personal and professional realms in ways that were beneficial. And so, through my grief I was able to use my heightened understanding of grief and loss to be more compassionate and decisive regarding myself and others. My self-work necessitated that I consider the facts before me, or if you like, the evidence of what was happening on the ground. I found myself drawing on those skills as a way of taking the action needed to bring balance and restoration to my family and myself.

This intertwining of my values, both personal and professional, also seemed to clarify my heightened awareness of a need to always try to be as authentic, realistic, kind and compassionate as I could. I was and am fulfilling my purpose with love and sincerity in my personal life; my professional life is becoming limited by choice. This widened understanding of my values and awareness was a gift and a way forward for me which I celebrated during those recovering years and which I continue to celebrate now.

As I reflected upon many of the people with whom I was involved (family, friends and others), I recognised that each one of them face what most of us experience at some time. That is, the confounding fact that most problems seemed encapsulated in physical, emotional or social frameworks. And of course, I recognised myself, as you might recognise yourself, within those sometimes-problematic frameworks. Quite often I, and possibly you, might have slipped into a loss of control. I lost control when I could not accept reality. As you might have. For a short time, I was not able to listen to another and compassionately understand their pain; I became subsumed into my world and could not concentrate on anyone else.

In the early days as a single young mother, I was ashamed of my predicament and could not perceive myself as worthy of self-compassion or friendship or love. Possibly my saving grace was that I did, eventually, look for opportunities to discuss my situation and I very quickly responded to the empathy and affection from family and friends who were offering support.

Subsequently, I have learnt many lessons about the strength of the human spirit and that we, you, me and all of us, wherever and whoever we are, will face some adversity throughout life. However, I realise that for some people who might think that they are incapable of enjoying what they have and instead mourn for what they do not have, a choice to consider oneself as enlightened, and humanised can be challenging. Some people can instead utilise savagery, ignorance or darkness to harm others in grievous ways and find relief in doing so. In doing so they are choosing to deny completeness of wellbeing for self or others. I believe that for some who might think they are incapable of enjoying what they do have, and mourning for what they do not have, say, contentment or peace in life, a choice to take charge of 'self' is nevertheless there.

We can either choose to learn and move forward to change a difficult life or possibly come to perceive that the difficulties will always be there to be suffered. Making choices for self can be inspiring, empowering and can positively change our lives. I recall hearing that Mahatma Ghandi was once asked what he thought of western civilisation and that his pithy response was something like, 'I think that would be a good idea'. I too think it would be a good idea to recall that civilisation simply means people all over the world progressing towards togetherness in spirit and in actuality. And many do achieve those high ideals – and many others are not aware of what a broad understanding of civilisation, togetherness for example, might mean. This seems to be a long-sought goal which does not seem to have ever been achieved in history or the present tumultuous virus-ridden world.

I needed to start small with my life and my community. As I progressed towards self-awareness and self-management, I was very open to the notion of discussing divisive conflict with either myself or others, to settle unhappy communications with a view to coming together towards reconciliation. I started by having conversations with myself.

You too can ask yourself to identify your most important issue or issues. You can further ask yourself to identify and recognise the emotions you attach to that issue. For example, desperation, antagonism, nervousness, powerlessness or anger versus peace, love or contentment. You could ask yourself to remember if and when you had experienced those emotions before and how you had handled those situations. You might reflect upon the emotional and limiting effects of being unable to excuse or forgive the other for real or imagined wrongs. You can encourage yourself to perceive that it is in your own self-interest to release those harmful, disruptive emotional ties. Those are questions and strategies that you can continue to utilise.

Positive movement occurred for me when I gently reminded myself that people with whom I could have been in conflict had, probably, not a care in the world about whether or not they had been forgiven and gave no thought to the importance of, or desire for, civil relations. I came to understand that it was only myself who continued to suffer through such unforgiving behaviour. Challenging and changing my long-held beliefs was a confronting task for me but change was critical in order to embrace, strengthen and otherwise value my own mental and physical health. You too can progress to meet those tasks in order to embrace, strengthen and value your own mental and physical health.

I choose, as indeed you might choose, to purposefully and steadfastly work to progress forward by practising joy, peacefulness, kindness, compassion and a loving attitude. You and I can acknowledge that those behaviours remain essential to progress: positive thoughts and positive behaviours go hand in hand. Positive behaviour after positive behaviour reinforces more positivity, increases resilience and promotes psychological growth.

You, your loved ones and others might always benefit, as I certainly do, from watching another discover the steps leading to roads forward. Movement forward sustains and allows you and I to enjoy personal hard-won growth. Each time a new way has birthed a vibrant new indication of forward movement for me, I know that through application and daily practise, such knowledge becomes indelibly part of who I am and how I am now living.

- *Take responsibility for your mindset and actions and have faith in your inner self. Make your own music and dance to your own tune. Plan your activities and believe in all forward-moving ideas. You can build internal power beyond measure.*

- *Keep growing forward and use humour and laughter as often as you have a chance. Put aside as far as possible gloom and doom scenarios. Be authentic and take it easy on yourself.*

- *As you move forward, assess how you are coping with your family, employment, friends, colleagues, and neighbourhood. When you feel that it is all coming together a little bit more each day, your sense of wellbeing will likely grow and your feelings will perhaps reflect more frequently your belief that you are worthwhile. You will be able to do more and more growing and tending to your life happiness goals.*

- *Always protect yourself from threats, imminent danger, long-term fear and cowering submission by developing the strength to make sound decisions that are beneficial to you and your loved ones.*

Chapter 7

Thinking About Life (and Justice?)

Following the loss of my son and the later loss of my grandson, I thought about questions I considered important and reflective of moving forward. In doing so, I was attempting to think logically and analytically about my life and the 'injustice', in real terms the down-to-earth reality, which had been stolen from each of my boys.

Since then, I have come to grasp that it is important to accept that we are designed to have the gift of this life for as long as we live. Not more, not less. This is the brutal truth and reality of human life. I have twice experienced and partially comprehended the terrible nature of murderous and accidental death and the misery and anguish that followed the losses of my boys. I look back through time and the notion of justice becomes irrelevant in actual reality. It seems irrelevant when faced with similar questions as to why certain people, worldwide, remain on the edge of desperation, poverty and decline and why sea turtles, for example, are dying in the seas due to climate- change.

The Sea Turtle Conservancy (Internet article 2021) reports that the atmospheric temperature is increasing as does the sand surrounding the eggs. As the temperature of the sand increases, more hatchlings will be female thereby skewing the ratio of females/males. There was a suggestion in the report that turtles may be an environmental indicator of the deadly impacts of global climate change. The turtles also face decimation because the plastic they eat, when they mistake and eat plastic for jelly fish, kills them. Turtles do not get to choose life or death. No justice available for sea creatures.

The way I now think about life and what I like to call 'justice' comes from my values, perceptions *and* my actions. I have at previous times been reduced to tatters and have experienced the loss of personal stoicism which I needed to rebuild in order to survive and endure. We all have our own fluidity of thought, personality and experience of self; I hypothesise that each person capable of reading this book is, to a very large extent, the product of his or her choices and that includes choices of thought processes. Do I hear you say "what!"?

Come to consider that your thoughts and thought processes are critical to you making choices that will benefit you and your life contentment. Are you a product of the choices you make, or of the way you consider your ongoing choices? Do you sink into a mire of despair from which you don't seem to be able to rise? Are you a thinking person who can understand that you can make self-beneficial choices and that no-one else can make those decisions for you in the way that you can? As you work forward in your practise of making decisions that will benefit your wellbeing, you will be growing self-responsibility and using same in your confidence and capacity to choose a plethora of ways to build positivity and self-reliance. Consider the phrase 'self-actualising'. Self-actualisation comes from the above; you and I might appreciate the reality our *actual* potential and the *actual* realisation and *actual* fulfilment of our movements forward into contentment which most of us seek throughout life.

However, on the other hand, if a brain is incapacitated to the extent that it's owner cannot formulate thoughts, then that person would not seem to be a product of his choices and thought processes which I consider would be tragic for that person and their loved ones. There are always exceptions to the rule as in the following story. I have read of one such exception – the challenging and heart-rending account of Martin Pistorius who suffered a disastrous brain infection at age 12. Over time this condition rendered him incapable of speech or voluntary movement. He had no physical capacity to indicate to his carers, or parents and other family members that his intellect was sound and that he was literally trapped inside his non-functioning body. Martin's story is one of the most poignant and brave life stories I have ever read. Years later he wrote a book *The Ghost Boy* published in 2009, after his massaging aromatherapist noticed what she thought was his capacity to respond to her friendly chatting to him. She considered he was answering her with his eyes and what minimal and indistinct movements he could produce. Her persistent interventions on his behalf birthed his now, many years later, contented and productive life. Read his book and be forever grateful for not suffering in the ways Martin described when he was defenceless and in extremely abusive day care. Read about his truly awe-inspiring movements forward over time as he taught himself to read and write, to use his alphabet board, his computer, his wonderful intellect and personality. Martin is now married and has a son with his beloved wife Joanna.

So therefore, always taking into account the exception to the rule, if I know who I am and I am cognitively aware, I have options regarding the way I choose to respond. You and I may have chosen to resist changing our less-than-useful responses by offering a long list of "I can't because" statements to ourselves in order to support our fear of and resistance to change. I knew that fear is markedly more powerful than pride and I also knew I could not choose to give way to fear of change. I aimed to always choose good solid mental health. I wanted to feel resilient and strong. I wanted to function well. I wanted to acknowledge gratitude for my life and benefits such as good health and a growing core of steadfast resilience.

As a result, I planned to work on small challenges at first. Like you I might have chosen to replace my ingrained automatic negative thoughts with 'I have another option'. I chose to build and strengthen new and old relationships. Like you, I could dance and exercise and make every attempt to avoid anxiety and sadness. As we can build and strengthen new ways of thinking so we can take on bigger challenges and, in doing so, work towards greater success at each stage. I chose to notice the positives and count all the reasons I had to be grateful.

I continue to love choosing to be happy. I choose to accept that harmony and similarly 'justice', worldwide, has never, in my understanding of history, existed. I understand that a healthy baby born to responsible, caring and loving parents in a 'free' country is simply fortunate. Others are not so fortunate. Taking responsibility for working with myself without clinging to 'I can't because' requires me to choose to be authentic, to shake off any residue of blaming another and to clearly realise that notions of fairness or equality for all, are simply just that: notions, ideas and wishes.

These are unique challenges for us. I remember one of my sociology lecturers saying that there is nothing quite like learning from, or watching, or listening to somebody who has walked a mile in the shoes in which you want to walk. I have learnt from and listened to those who have assisted others to move forward.

For example, I saw on television an illuminating but brief interview showing a father and a little girl of perhaps about three years of age. The child's father had, he said, tried to enable her happiness by offering her a positive experience rather than naming war bombings and inciting trauma. He explained to whomever was videoing the interview that there was no possibility of escape from his situation. He encouraged his little girl to hear the falling bombs around their home in a war-torn country, as fireworks. The child was shown laughing as she bounced on an old couch and as she became excitedly happy when she heard the "fireworks". I admired his extraordinary imagination and thoughtfulness towards his little girl as he strived to encourage her to be happy. He did not mention injustice or justice, or the utter devastation and absurd, cruel loss of life in war, he did not choose to live in unhappiness and he delighted in trying to ensure the child's happiness. He did not complain about why he and his daughter were in that predicament or express any expectation of justice from the situation. He had accepted that there was little to do but to care for and help his child.

So, what to do? You must remain staunchly determined to enjoy your life without the weight of unfairness upon your mind and your life. You will be here be here, as I will be here, for such a short time; we are born and we die. Nevertheless, I have what I value, some freewill and capacity to enjoy, influence and decide my choices for forward thinking. You must value your freewill to do the same.

I always remember reading about and looking up to Nelson Mandela as an icon of a selfless, endlessly strong and humane man. I read his story in his book *The Long Walk Home*, wherein he chose to be the man he was. He later became President, despite his devastating twenty-seven years in prison. I still enjoy re-reading his inspiring life story. Mr Mandela suffered torment, cruel and inhumane treatment, anguish and depression. It took twenty-seven years for this now-deemed innocent man to be released from prison.

During those years, his beloved son died and Mr Mandela was refused the right to attend his funeral. Mr Mandela noted his own efforts to have others perceive him as another human being and one who lived with patience and positivity. He complained to those who were in charge of his prison conditions that he, in contrast with the white prisoners, had to sleep on the cold concrete without pyjamas. His requests for pyjamas were, reportedly, denied. Here was a man who must have had great personal strength and courage to choose ways to survive the sinister and inhumane ways with which he was dealt.

And so, in comparison to the life tragedies that some face, I believe now and believed then, that my choices present me with ways of thinking that might challenge my other less useful ways of thinking. You too must build your choices and build your own repertoire of ideas and movements forward. Please don't consider justice or injustice to have impacted your life. We can look back through history to see that life and justice over the long and unhurried trickle of time has fairly well lacked worldwide social inclusion of all those who do not seem to be one of us. We seem to have capacity to demean, ignore, hate, kill and otherwise mistreat some people seen as quite different from us. We may consider ourselves above or distant from those who are perceived to be less deserving. They could be called the Other. And that is how it has been since time immemorial and clearly that is how it remains. The Other could be the dead on the war field, or those dying of COVID, for example, where treatments are not available.

The Other might be those who do not look like us, or who may have a different language or colour for example. The capacity to act with kindness in true and honourable ways remains within each of us to determine.

For the most of us, we seem to create and further our own 'justice' and enhance our lives by remaining constant. I believe, like we all might believe, that I can influence my circumstances through hard work and by making choices that benefit my life and, importantly, harm no-one. I try to be at one with myself throughout. There is no absolute right or wrong way to perceive life. My way, as does your way for you, needs to work for me without causing others pain, in contrast, by trying to bring happiness to myself and in my wake. I write positive things each day as I learn to identify and seek out my strengths and I practise using my strengths as often as is practical, which is nearly always. I try to practise unplanned acts of kindness with whomever I encounter; I enjoy the positive emotions that come with greeting and possibly helping another.

As you might, I also like to work towards doing what I can to contribute to others' wellbeing whilst building my own firm, strong and persistent platform of personal happiness and contentment. I cannot benefit all of those in need with just and appropriate outcomes, for example, by solving climate change difficulties, or eliminating mass starvation or cruel and demeaning racism issues, or the myriad of injustices we see the world facing. I can, however, do what I can in my little world.

We too can come to appreciate the absolute frailty and the preciousness of life. We might recognise our fragility when we have treated others inconsiderately or inattentively or when we momentarily slide back into sad memories. We can strive to perceive the world as it really is. We can be committed, as everyone might be committed, to continue to change and enhance the track of our thoughts, intentions, purpose and promise. We need to choose, meditate, believe, and find pathways forward into happiness for ourselves and for our loved ones.

I enjoy and value my life, as you might, as I have described. I do not look for equality for all as in believing in a harmonious and virtuous society. I perceive such a society to be an improbability: maybe just a whistling in the wind. So, if I am in need of good cheer and positivism I can talk to a friend, or walk in the parks around our area, as I am sure you might choose to do. I can introduce my mind to a wider panorama of thoughts, interests, beliefs and movements. I can delve into offering help anywhere and whenever it's possible. I choose to work towards a deeper understanding of the meaning and import of my everyday life, everyday interactions, ideals and beliefs and my own respective goals. These can be your goals as well.

Most of us strive for the freedom of happiness. These freedoms make up some of my goals. I know that I have experienced overwhelming anguish, which I accept will always remain in my memory, as I live with the loss of my boys. Nevertheless, I want to live life to its full completeness, to continue my happiness goals. If the opportunities arise, I will do what I can for others to achieve the same goals.

So, I think of a red rose. I can imagine the beautiful red petals are velvet to the touch. I can imagine sipping a glass of Veuve Clicquot champagne (or the best one we can afford) with my life friend and husband over a simple fresh dinner in the comfort of our home. If I can imagine and stay focussed on the rose or other pleasant thoughts, then I can, simply, change the track of my meditations. Breathing in and breathing out, I am watching the red rose as I relax further into my bed; I am purposefully creating new and stronger thinking. The more I do this, the more I move in that direction; the more I do this, the easier it becomes for me to sleep peacefully.

Whoever and wherever I have been at my worst point of negativity, I will not be in the future. You too can strive to adopt this promise to yourself.

- *In this society and in this time, strive for your goals. They may be myriad and may include hopes for peace, love and happiness. Do what you can to resolve any unfairness that you perceive. Always cling to your own personal goodness, kindness and willing spirit.*

- *I believe the quality of internal harmony and mind-peace could be centred in each individual's soul. Find your inner strength and strive for internal harmony and peace each day.*

- *Abandon and dismiss any doubt that you can walk forward into happiness. Keep your goals in front of your movements and thoughts, and experience success as you do so.*

• *You and I can benefit from building inner strength and quality of character. Try putting aside any belief that your values are unimportant; we base our behaviours on our values, we see all of nature as being part of life. You might understand that humanity is part of life in the world, both the physical and the mystical.*

• *We do not need rules or justice to make us breathe in and breathe out and in the same way we do not need a rule or a legal-ethical urging to live in happiness. I, for example, believe happiness is a natural and human gift for each of us if we choose to work towards same. Who do we consider is responsible for giving us the gift of happiness? You and I are the 'givers' of happiness to ourselves.*

Chapter 8

Finding Acceptance

P eter and I loved Luke and we continue to celebrate and love our memories of him. He was generous and affectionate and he enjoyed spending time with us. We shared great times. Luke was an outdoors boy and man. At the time of this tragedy, that is, the killing of Luke, he had his son James living with him. James was a bright and happy little boy who had been fortunate enough to live with his father after his half-siblings had been taken into care. I recall going to Luke's house to return James to his home one evening. Luke had just finished doing the dishes and James proudly and happily went to put away the dishes in the cupboards and drawers telling us that this was his daily job.

Luke liked to walk in the nearby countryside as often as he could and he always took James with him. They had two dogs to walk and care for and Peter and I sometimes went with them. When James was about seven years of age, just prior to his coming to live with us, his father bought him a little motorbike which James learned to ride. We would watch him with no small amount of trepidation and simultaneous love and pride.

On one occasion, James rode into a low-hanging branch and fell off the bike. Luke, who was a bit overweight, huffed and puffed as he sprinted to pick James up and to check if he was okay. James was unhurt and wanted to ride again but motorbike riding was done for the day. I remember the day especially because we were all very happy.

After, when James went to school to 'show and tell,' he spoke to the class about the motorbike present from his dad. Some of the children were not inclined to believe him. After speaking with the teacher, Luke put the little bike on the trailer and took it to school for another show and tell. James was so happy and proud and he and his father laughed for days at the amazed looks on the children's faces. I treasure our times together and can now relive such memories and stories with comfort and joy.

I remember the terrible deadly assault upon Luke like it was yesterday. It was very late at night when I was already asleep. Peter came into the bedroom waking me. He told me that he had heard from Luke's friend that Luke had been attacked violently and that Luke did not seem to have a pulse. In rapidly escalating shock and horror, we immediately drove to the place where Luke had been attacked.

We passed an ambulance coming out of the street in which Luke lived. I ran over to them. The vehicle stopped and I asked the paramedics if Luke was the patient. The looks on their faces told me all I needed to know. They looked at each other and did not say anything other than that they did not have any patient in the ambulance.

When we arrived at the dreadful scene, I was certain that Luke was dead but knew equally as absolutely that he might, perhaps, maybe, could possibly still be alive. After threading our way through the cordoned-off street, we could see there were bright police spotlights everywhere but especially in front of the house. I saw a body lying on the ground covered by a sheet and I still believed it must be a mistake. The police did not try to stop me. I remembered thinking right then and there that the mind can be a very protective shield against reality at times. I ran and knelt down next to Luke. I pulled the sheet back to see his face and wished he would wake up. I was crying out his name and when I discovered I was kneeling in his blood, I cried even harder. I cannot actually remember what I did or said or felt. I was numb, frozen, in a twilight world. Peter tells me I called Luke's name over and over and that I leant over to kiss him. Peter and the police tried to draw me away. I cannot remember what Luke looked like at that time. I recalled learning that the brain is composed of billions and billions of working parts and that it can accept numerous facts per second. I now also believe that a brain can exercise equally-powerful strategies to bury information and facts that the brain's owner cannot process in that moment. I am glad that protective shield remains in place to this day. When I later heard of Luke's extensive and fatal injuries, I was rooted to the spot. I could not comprehend and did not want to think of how he must have suffered until his death.

The whole thing was surreal. Amazing, horrifying, savage, unbelievable, no chance of life surviving. Even so, I could not stop from thinking that it was still a mistake. Even in the face of seeing him lying there on the concrete without breathing and without moving I still blindly waited for it not to be so.

I was walking inside where the police wanted to ask us questions. You might have heard the expression 'I was shocked out of my brain'. That was me. I cannot remember if I spoke any sense to the detectives or not. I remember Amanda, one of the detectives, asking me questions. I have no idea what I said to her. Peter appeared steadfast but crushed and although just as affected as I, he was able to answer questions put to him. We did not have any answers that could help the police. We were utterly confused, heartbroken, unbelieving, traumatised and stunned into silence.

I simply could not believe that his neighbour had not heard anything or had not come out to help him. I could not believe that Luke had not been able to let his two dogs out to scare away the intruders. I came up with so many possible scenarios which could have occurred in order to have extinguished the already end result of death.

That night we sat in the house until morning so as not to take our dear little boy James through the dreadful brightly-lit scene outside. I could not tell you what we did or said for those hours. We went to sit by James's bed and waited for him to wake up. We gently told James his father had died. We explained that he was coming home with us. James cried as he nestled into our arms. He too looked dumbfounded, shocked, scared and lost. I can only believe that any child like James has no framework or point of reference to make any sense of such a traumatic event.

We packed up some of James's things and Peter wrapped him in a quilt and carried him outside. Luke's body was gone by then but James stared over Peter's shoulder at the blood-stained ground.

We called Luke's very good friend who, without hesitation, came to take charge of the house and the dogs. His generosity in that moment was something we will always remember. He cried as much as we did and continued to visit in the future to see little James. James loved those visits when he was taken to visit his very large dog which had been adopted by another of Luke's friends who had a large backyard. We had no such backyard.

Peter's daughter Georgia my stepdaughter and her former partner supported us in every way we could have wished. They were towers of strength in our hour of need as were each and every other family member of the two of us.

I have written earlier about my struggle towards regaining mental strength, brick by mental brick, wherein I could benefit myself, James and Peter. I needed to try to cease thinking about Luke's death for the very simple reason that no-one, no intervention, absolutely no anything, could change any aspect of what had occurred. Then and now. Quite often in those early days following Luke's death, I would wake up crying out for him. After many months of reframing my thoughts, examining and reflecting, I came to imagine, consciously, that he was now part of the universe, just not part of this living world. I am at peace with that interpretation.

As previously described, the police detectives located the offenders and they were tried in a criminal court. They were found guilty and sentenced to prison. As I look back, I understand that the above processes of sought justice were and remain almost irrelevant to me now. I have not met or heard of, or from, anyone who has ever been able to reverse such events, or reshape the death of an individual, or rebuild, or return one single person who has already died.

Luke's funeral was one wherein the largest chapel and linked areas were packed with family and Luke's and our friends. People were standing around the walls as there were no seats left. Following, his ashes were placed quite near to his maternal grandparents' place of rest. Nobody knew what to say to us about Luke's loss except to say he had been a great friend to many. All offered their heartfelt condolences.

I was already determining, and intellectually knew, that I must change my attitude from grief and introspection. I didn't want to find myself behaving in any counterproductive way which might arise from ignoring or disavowing my discovered 'freedom of choice' thoughts. My attitude needed to change to avoid such renouncement of purpose and the possibly ensuing and endlessly-self-defeating thoughts and behaviours. I needed to work towards building a positive attitude and constructive thought processes. I needed to pretend, if necessary, at any point that I was okay and would in the very close future be 'getting there'. I needed to hold firmly

Chapter 12

Self-worth

It took me a long hard walk up the road to have discovered that the above qualities are absolutely critical to life happiness. An abundance of each of the above welcome qualities paves my way with emotional gold. I don't stop to ask myself if my brain and mental strength are up to the task; I rejoice in the idea that self-worth is an amalgamation of the above qualities of self-acceptance, self-love and self-esteem. I do not choose to have continuous thoughts of negativity about myself. I understand that self-esteem is a strong platform for life-happiness-seeking and I pretty well always enjoy choosing a vision of my internal glass being full. I have finally let go of fears real or imagined. This is an important chapter – read it a number of times as you reflect upon how you perceive yourself.

This book is an expose of my strategies and the tactics I have taken to move forward. I am hopeful that I will never give up on the future and I am continuously grateful for all of those I am privileged to love and enjoy. My thinking and acceptance of what life has brought and will bring to my table provides the way of my choices, for happiness and for self-love. I hope never to choose self-destructive behaviour in any way, shape or form. Quite the opposite, I choose and plan to be as fully functioning as my mind and body will provide so that I can also choose to live in the now moment, fully and consciously, of every waking moment. I can choose to evolve into authenticity or choose to remain shackled to fear, negative judgement and, or perhaps, stagnancy. The latter states of mind, I find, do not encourage any person, you or me, to become fully conscious or realised.

I am also living a peaceful life in harmony with others, where I both create and discover different approaches forward to happiness when I accept myself with love and positivity. I used to ask myself, 'Do you really think you can do this?' and I would answer, 'No problem, just give it a go'. And gradually I have come to believe that self-acceptance leads to more resilience of mind and spirit. I have spoken of the loss of my loved son and grandson and I have accepted that their deaths were twice-occurring crises for me. But I have chosen not to be powerless or shattered by external events, or unspeakable circumstances. I choose to work extremely hard to reaffirm my present and future happiness state and take every chance to build personal resilience in order to maintain a joyful and meaningful life happiness.

But, in the first instance, I struggled to understand that self-awareness, thinking logically and being coherent, were keys to a strong base for self-acceptance, self-esteem, self-worth and self-love. I tried to work from that base knowing that I had no choice but to follow through with the above strategies if I wanted to live a life apart from distress and pain and sorrow. Over time, I think I have mostly succeeded in utilising and growing my self-awareness and self-worth. I continue to practise growing accustomed to enhancing interactions with others, and to identify with myself as a person with knowledge of how to be honest with myself and others. I have applied myself to mental and psychological growth and still find that I am coming to know myself as a person who really concentrates on being aware of what is happening in my head. With such self-awareness, throughout my life-long journey towards contentment, I seem to be better aware of my and others' actions and responses, musings, ideas, feelings, and purpose. My resulting thoughts seem to reflect my insights and I can practise doing what I do in both self-rewarding and self-predictive ways.

Self-esteem, arrived at through mindful choices and methodical focus on self-truth and true self-reality, can only enrich an individual's positioning in the happiness stakes. That is true for you and me. Regard for self and others and taking personal responsibility to act towards self and others, can only enhance our self-esteem. This means we must intentionally contemplate and focus on reality, hold commitment to, and regard for our own egos, and constantly engage in supportive and restorative thoughts. One of my realities is that I am only 155 centimetres tall; I need steps to reach nearly anything up high. Another is that I burn to a crisp in the direct sunlight, and I am getting wrinkles! I am a human being and I can only accept and delight that I am as fortunate as I am. I am in excellent health and overall, I am happy with myself, both physically and mentally.

There is not much in the natural world that I can't appreciate. On the other hand, some painful phenomena exist and always have existed in the human world. For example: I understand that the entire Earth's population experiences a pitiless divide between those with privilege and those without. The 'with-outs' might experience violence, racism, pain, hunger, imprisonment and suffering of any nature as well as cultivated cruelty as in war. I can only accept that those things have been with us since time immemorial and always will be in existence. I do what I can against such blights which have always been with us. I can help others and I do. I can argue against injustice and I do so when I can. But I do not allow things I cannot change to alter my perception of myself as being worthy, valuable, creditable, and committed to my internal inclinations. And neither should you allow any of those things to alter your perception of yourself as worthy.

Hope and optimism help you and me to weather the emotional storms and upheavals we might face. Flexible optimists, those with self-esteem and knowledge of their self-worth, can bounce, rebound, renew, and replace pessimism with a different strategy, the strategy of talking to and dealing with oneself. A flexible optimist can prepare, think, plan and be illuminated by an awareness as he or she encourages the self to take a number of actions. You and I can avoid sitting in a mire of self-sorrow and unhappiness but instead seek out positivity. You and I can think of every success we have ever had; the tiniest little success is a very welcome opportunity to celebrate moving forward. Optimism is a free attribute for all, particularly for those who work hard to stay in the frame.

Self-sorrow and unhappiness are links in the chain of stress factors. Stress has been described as a behaviour altering factor in that we might eat more than we need, weigh more than we should, and smoke more in the face of evidence revealing the death-dealing nature of the habit. Stress might lead you or I to hate what we believe we cannot change or avoid, and to sit, sit and sit as we commiserate with ourselves. I have bordered on the edges of being shut down by stress. I knew that was not where I wanted to be.

Responses must be strategised. Fear should be ostracised and, instead, mindful strategies developed. The practise of meditation, exercise, yoga, walking, going to the gym, swimming, eating healthily, consuming minimal alcohol, keeping an eye on your blood pressure, cholesterol levels, and a good night's sleep are all mindful strategies. Your practises provide benefits to your mind and body and are to be celebrated every day.

A reduction in stress is so good for our bodies, blood pressure reduces, meditation and fruit teas replace use of alcohol and our pulse lowers its rate. These changes to the bodily state, are likely to be reflected in your state of mind and significant improvement in mood and temperament. There could be, then, a repetitive and welcoming turn around in what you desire to eat, drink and how you care for your body. Such planned choices start to reflect your improved emotional state and your healthier choices, all of which feed back into your higher wellbeing and happier state of mind.

- *Planning to and preparing for self-action requires action now – and an understanding that you cannot continue as you are if indeed you are feeling despairing, unloved, unaccepted and unworthy.*

- *Therefore, you need to build a defence against being afraid of the dark. Our fears can be really debilitating. Think about what is available to you to examine possible solutions. Write a list and tick off all that you can immediately deal with.*

- *Determine confirmation of your positive ideas, your acceptance of self as a person worthy of your and others' love, and worthy of your own self-esteem. Know that you are able to move forward, talk to yourself, to your trusted family and friends, or to a therapist, a counsellor or other.*

- *Write your list of plans, get ready for action, go for gold in treating yourself with love and compassion. List your memories of times when you have conquered a fear, given yourself praise for being confident, or when another person has been helped by your assistance and friendship.*

- *Rejoice in the tiniest steps forward – you are on your way! Take charge of your very unique and special self, revel in your strength of purpose and always keep on keeping on.*

CHAPTER 13

Strategic Action

The information in this book does not have a mythical God's eye view. It represents just some of the multiplicities of the meaning of happiness. But throughout these chapters, happiness has been viewed as a primary goal in achieving a different way of life, a happiness way that every day in this moment you and I can choose for our*selves*.

I have benefitted from my strong loving relationship with Peter. I have multiple benefits from enjoying, then and remembering now, my boys. I am fortunate with having an important array of loving family members and friends. I have welcomed the gifts of education and wide-ranging work experiences. I have faced extreme sorrows with the death of my only son and his only son. I have needed to challenge and escape the potential death of my positive outlook on life. I fell over but also knew that I was the person to build, for myself, as you are for yourself, a firmer and long-lasting positive outlook on life.-

What was and is true for me is no different than what is

true for you and most of humankind. The world, as I knew it prior to the loss of my boys, disappeared before my eyes. I acknowledge, as you can acknowledge, that life-changes are ever present, rapid and possibly alarming at times. I knew that I could not wait for my world to return to normality by some magical process. I could not expect things to return to the way they were without strength and without making good choices, as indeed you cannot. I could not miss the rest of my life, as you should not, by waiting for Godot.

I needed to become even more attached to mindfulness. I needed to become increasingly robust and more accepting of unexpected death. I wanted to become stronger against recurring thoughts of tragedy and misfortune. That has become my every-day mindset. Mostly, I wanted and continue to want to work towards my life goals, the happiness project is definitely for me and for as many others as I can positively influence.

So, to repeat the strategies that I continue to use. Firstly, I focussed on my physical and mental health. I determined to exercise every day, I continue to do my exercise classes and walk between seven thousand five hundred and mostly more than ten or more thousand steps a day. I eat fresh food, mainly fish, fruit and vegetables. I enjoy small amounts of red meat and chicken dishes are a favourite. The less alcohol the better.

In combination with the above, the most important strategy is to choose one's own mindset and determine to follow positivity with an abundance of self-esteem, self-direction, self-worth and all other self-enhancing strategies. In that way

I could work, as you can work, assiduously towards happiness goals. I had to take responsibility, as the late Professor Emeritus Zygmunt Baumann might say, to be personally responsible for my own well-being, choices and behaviours without relying on any other directive voice. Taking responsibility to be personally responsible for self-authenticity and self-direction is an essential characteristic to adopt for each of us. I am fortunate to believe in mind training, to welcome learning new strategies each day and to gain the benefits of seeking, appreciating, living and loving the happiness in every living moment. I take personal responsibility for my happiness goals. You too can practise and develop taking personal responsibility for your happiness, wellbeing, good health, contentment and development of sound, rewarding relationships.

I speculate that many people might perceive my experiences of loss as heartrending. I agree they were. But humankind has always faced loss, grief and tragedy. Worldwide disasters abound. I can only respond with even more compassion, sensitivity and kindness.

Another most important strategy I always stress, as you will have noticed, is the use of meditation. I have found my style of meditation and I have read as many books as I could find about practising meditation. Mostly, I continue to use meditation to relax and enjoy a good night's sleep. I focus on my breathing, inhaling and exhaling. I focus on any beautiful thought and dismiss any intrusion of sad or other unhappy thoughts. I mentally list some of the beautiful day's events, thoughts and happenings I have enjoyed and use those thoughts at night in a meditative way. I do not choose pain in any form. I realise I choose different strategies at different times. As I search for and adapt my meditations, I underline my own individualistic steps I have come to enjoy.

Another important and ever-present strategy, from my perspective, is to hold a firm belief in my capacity to heal and make personal change. Can you develop such a perspective? My strength of purpose is also critical; I also realise fear, doubt and indecision are the enemies of my practised courage and purposefulness. Every healing thought I focus on and grant to myself is knitted into my search for happiness, for me and for those I love and also for others. Of course, I have much work to do over time. I take care and time to welcome the work, welcome the struggle and continue to desire the outcome of enjoying lifelong happiness. You will be pleasantly surprised how your mood will improve as you strive to work towards your own search for happiness, self-respect and contentment. I have researched myself and pinpointed the reasons that I am able to smile and be happy. You can also pinpoint your reasons and outcomes. Simplicity wins over complexity, what makes me happy, who makes me happy, are simple understandings but indeed my way forward. And good meditation material! Get to know all of those things about yourself and enjoy!

Go to your library or community centre and ask the librarians or community staff for the most popular books or other information about meditation. There are different types of meditation, I like mindfulness meditation, loving-kindness meditation and listening to guided meditation via a compact disc or through (in Australia), Headspace. The basic techniques of meditation usually commence with you finding a quiet and calm spot where you can practise your breathing and focus your concentration. You will find great books at the library to utilise and you can try each type until you find some that particularly suit you.

Through meditation, I find I am in charge each and every day and you can be too. I can choose to practise self-happiness each day as I live my life by choosing to dispense with self-crushing behaviour. I actively am aware not to allow any person, movie, book or news item to dirty or muddy my positive outlook. I manage to take control of my thoughts and I mentally change the subject if my thoughts are negatively swayed by any of the above 'dirty' communications. I choose new, positive, self-enhancing thoughts! I have made this sound so very easy, and it is of course, in contrast, very hard work. But rest assured the harder and longer you work at this mind-state, the easier it becomes. Meditation is an excellent resource.

My strategies are neatly encapsulated into the present moment. This present moment is the moment you and I are in and always will be. I continue to work, as you can work, to focus on authenticity rather than triviality. I choose not to hide behind carefully-constructed disguises as you too might choose not to do and I additionally avoid playing games in any relationship.

I value openness and present myself as I see myself. I take care to maintain all loving personal and family relationships because they are so important to me. I try hard not to influence others but instead might ask encouragingly how a person might seek their own way forward. I do not find pleasure, amusement or benefit in wounding or correcting others in any way that could further their unhappiness.

I focus on my pursuit of happiness, again in the present moment. This is the right time, right now. I know living in the past is a mistake. I know time gone by is irrecoverable. In this moment of choice, I can be living my life as I wish. And I do not necessarily look only towards the pleasures of tomorrow. Tomorrow might never come. This moment is the time for me, I cannot impress upon you the importance of this moment. I choose to repetitiously practise living in this present moment. My practise and repetition require strength and concentration; my thoughts are my own as your thoughts are your own. I encourage myself to promote my feeling of control over my everyday life; I believe in myself as I keep on making deliberate movements towards happiness.

- *Strategies abound, simply start thinking about making choices. Determine your mind is your own. Your choices are for you to make; always remember that ways forward will be available to you.*

- *Choose to live healthily, choose to act with integrity, choose to act with compassion, know yourself to be honest and kind, energetic and fruitful, passionate and purposeful.*

- *Practise your meditation every day. Strategies abound, start with self, you in this moment and how and why you are choosing to do what you do.*

- *Ask yourself the critical questions, why are you doing something that makes you angry, sad, frustrated, in pain, feeling useless, chronically nauseous or ineffective? Or why are you feeling powerless, small, afraid, ineffective, unhappy, cruel, violent, slightly insane, or selfish and full of hate? Meditate all negativity away. Work towards changing what you can.*

- *Go forward. Put aside fear, practise meditation, yoga, deep breathing, get a massage.*

- *Delight in the following: lay in the warmth of the sun, enjoy the rain, feel the wind, look at the leaves and the birds. Talk to yourself comfortingly and kindly, treasure your movements forward.*

- *Watch the passing parade of people walking their dogs, listen to the chatter of those around you, smile at everyone you meet, respond happily to their chats and presence.*

- *Go to the library and get a really good book about love and kindness, read about people who have overcome enormously difficult life challenges like paraplegia, stroke, disabling accidents and so on.*

- *Be grateful for your health and your life; it is the only one you will get.*

- *Practise gratitude every day. Be grateful if you have a bed to sleep in and for your body to sleep in the bed. It is the only body you will ever have. Be grateful for your parents who birthed you; if they did not then you would not be here to complain.*

- *Choose not to complain, determine and remain determined to work really hard at making step by step pathways forward, build your brick-by-brick mental steps to take with you into the outer edges of happiness and from there into your own individual idea of life happiness and from there into your future garden of a happy life.*

CHAPTER 14

Discovery of Self

A s I mentioned previously, the heart-rending injustice of death, of loss and of ensuing pain is visible worldwide. In contrast, contented happiness for all humankind is not as easily visible. But, as I have realised, this is not to say you or I have to blindly accept such pain. I do and have done whatever I could to push back irrelevant questions about what 'could have been'. If I had not moved forward in my thinking, and away from the tide of grief and sadness relating to the death of my boys, I would have been failing myself and them.

When I open wide my 'living with acceptance' eyes, I understand that wishing for what was is part of the journey towards going past the limits of ongoing grief and reaching recognition of what is, an affirmative feedback loop; I let go and replace the black magnet that draws me towards tension or pain. I erase, in my mind, all negativity, pain or sadness that is captured by the black magnet and free my mind to build new, positive and peaceful pain-free thoughts and plans.

Fairness of life events for each and every one of us is simply not a reality for the majority of human beings in this universe. I am practical when I compassionately cite to myself the unchangeable, I do not have control over my gender, the colour of my eyes, my white privileged racial grouping, or the death of my loved ones through deliberate cruel action by others and through accident. I have discovered, nevertheless, aspects of action over which I did and do take control. I now do not surrender my thoughts to overwhelming grief or sadness. You too can determine not to surrender your thoughts to grief or sadness or angry bitterness.

I acknowledge and remind myself of the massive and tragic losses of life in the world, not only through accident, but through illness, war or suicide or other 'new normal' death-dealing traumas. There appear to be more viruses and more earthquakes, fires and floods and never-ending decades of war. I accept the emergence of my 'new normal' that is, living with, and accepting the loss of Luke and James. I recognise, concede and welcome the fact that the 'new normal' nevertheless hinges upon my willingness to embrace life's opportunities for personal and relationship happiness.

These thoughts and this knowledge were always available to me. I knew that my actions needed to closely link and reflect living with hope and rationality. I needed to deal with myself and other people with patience, care, compassion and kindness. Rather than looking around and being jealous of others who might have what I have lost; that is, the promise of those two loving relationships, I needed to work towards acceptance. I need to continue to acknowledge that envy is a wasteful emotion which goes hand in hand with 'it isn't fair'. I hold close the thought that success in any venture is simply committing to and doing my best with authenticity of purpose.

In the end, I need to stay upbeat to work tirelessly towards acceptance and simultaneously forget the events surrounding Luke's death by wilful, purposeful killing. I do not actually think of those persons at all, I must say, in terms of forgiveness or otherwise. I have heard arguments that if any accused person is so affected by alcohol or drugs then he or she may not have been able to form the intention to kill. I understand those arguments but resile from them. At the same time, I also believe under-privileged people may never have had opportunities to empathise, or feel part of a close, loving family or community. I will never be called upon to regard the perpetrators of Luke's death in any particular way or to speak with or relate to them. And that's fine with me. I know that now they are out there living their lives after years in prison. Again, I understand that acceptance of what is, rather than what could or might have been, is a necessary state of mind for any of us to get on with life and contentment. And, of course, that means the perpetrators of such murderous death must also, if they wish for a life they can enjoy, strive to go past their crimes and imprisonment and discover and build alternate lives.

I have finished with questions about why. What is evident and unchangeable is that both the manslaughter and the motorbike accident occurred. I choose to accept those inalienable facts in order to choose happiness and contentment instead of focussing on the things that can never change. Each one of us is an imperfect human; perfection is simply not possible.

So, I believe in myself, my imperfections and in my feelings and my actions. I firmly believe that my behaviours and deliberate actions have consequences for my wellbeing and for that of those around me. I believe in hope and goal setting, laughter, mindfulness, meditation and trust. I believe in love, kindness and compassion and I hold belief in my thus far earnt achievements. I have described how my education and subsequent privileges gained in the human service work areas have encouraged and informed me regarding choices of positivity in actions. They have gifted me choices in treating others with belief in the quality of humaneness and with respect, honour and open-handedness. These qualities I believe are critical to being able to appreciate others' qualities, the beauty of each day, and the present moment. I enjoy the blue sky which presents a different picture to us every day and night. The sky reminds me of each individual's thoughts, including mine. The sky and our thoughts are everchanging but are constantly there. They are similar in that our thoughts are always fluctuating, similarly to the sky. The sky presents us with a different array of clouds, or sunshine or stormy weather, every day and night.

I like to think that as the clouds and all cosmic bodies wander through the sky, so do our thoughts wander through our minds. You and I can enjoy and benefit from an everchanging panorama of possibilities for our lives. I will never have it all worked out, never, but I will certainly make it my happy business to keep seeking joy and contentment and that is all I need. I understand the sky will keep metamorphosing for as long as this world exists. I trust that I too will keep becoming for as long as I exist.

- *Some ideas to go on with*

- *I have experienced many things in my life as I have described. I have overcome much and have found many ways by which I have altered my perceptions of the past.*

- *You can ask yourself those same questions about how to enjoy your life and use those same strategies. What is it that you want? Can you strategise a pathway to achieve your goals?*

- *Define your goals, keep your lists, write as many ways to achieve your goals as you can find. Work hard on your tasks.*

- *Do not look for magic or fantasies for healing. Choose your memories and the filters through which you view those memories. You can now believe that truths are simply the facts.*

- *Carefully choose your filters to clarify a fact as, simply, how things really are.*

- *Be selective when sorting through your memories, reject those that bring pain or strife to your mind.*

- *Acknowledge the way forward is to face reality, 'what is' rather than 'what could be' or 'should be' or 'might be'.*

- *You can choose to place very little limitation in your ways forward to happiness. There is nothing to fear from your thoughts regarding seeking contentment and making sound choices. You can always find joy in your memories of the good times you remember. Do not seek out sad thoughts, ask yourself what purpose would there be in seeking sad thoughts?*

- *Look for courage and safety rather than considering fear. Choose not to grieve. Rather, pursue bright consciousness and look for other positive ways to bring consolation and relief from inexpressible pain or grieving. Your future life possibilities are waiting for you, they could be active and radiant with the energy of happiness. You can spread out and expand your comfort zone and you can be still and tranquil in peaceful reflection.*

- *Search for that light inside yourself where you absolutely believe in yourself. Believe in self so that you can put aside any fears, doubts or thoughts that you cannot find a path forward to happiness. Be resilient and grateful to yourself for your self-directed life always.*

- *When you experience grievous loss, distress, ruptured relationships, violence or psychological and emotional abuse, you then have true understanding of your life's immeasurable value. Be grateful for such understanding and work towards making change. Please note the organisations at the beginning of the book.*

- *If you have true understanding, you can authenticate your purpose and pathways. Be grateful for your authenticity.*

- *Keep on your chosen path in order to keep expanding, growing, loving, liking, seeking, questioning, meditating and living with joy and peace. Refuse falling into sadness or being afraid.*

- *Choose to live in a position where belief, wellbeing, richness of spirit and goodness highlight your days. Be happy, keep coming into yourself as you walk freely and confidently forward into your life happiness.*

www.ingramcontent.com/pod-product-compliance
Lightning Source LLC
Chambersburg PA
CBHW032058020426
42335CB00011B/403